YOU COULDN'T MAKE THIS UP!

Secret Diaries of a Secondary School Teacher

MARK MACDONALD

Dedicated to Rocio
B & J & KJ

Table of Contents

Exit Insult

In my first school job after completing my teacher training, PGCE, I found myself on a split site school. For the afternoon lessons, which were normally more boisterous and difficult to handle, I had a fractious group of Year 11 pupils on a Tuesday and Friday afternoon. These students had probably had a string of supply teachers before, because of the shortage of science teachers and the general difficulty recruiting. They had lost a lot of focus let's say.

I started one lesson I thought quite well, with a short video clip of various fireworks and hoping to link that to the relative colours of different elements when they burn. We were going to do simple flame tests. It was a low ability group. However not long into the lesson an argument broke out about something that had happened at lunchtime break between a group of lads. Another reason afternoon sessions could be more edgy!

Even in this Catholic school, many swear words were allowed to pass, otherwise no work would ever have been done. Obviously the exceptions being blaspheming, or using the F word or C word, as in see you next Tuesday.

A couple of boys were swearing at each other and one was using the belligerent sounding F word. F**K. Which is what I thought. Got to deal with this.

I had to intervene. The prevailing practice was to ask the student to leave the class, stand outside the door, until there was a suitable pause in the lesson, so that the teacher could pop out and 'have a word' with the miscreant away from his or her audience. The other advantage was that the rest of the class didn't know what was said outside the room. All going well, the troublemaker could be let back into the class, suitably chastened hopefully, or not as the case may be. Some students needed a quiet word, some needed a bit of a rollicking.

If a teacher got the wrong approach, then it usually made the situation very much worse!

I asked Jack to leave the class as he had used the F word. Not directed at me, but at one of the other boys. As he churlishly shoved back his stool. He scraped the stool's feet on the parquet floor and began to stride passed me out of the classroom, he let rip another F word at his classmates, who were snickering and goading him as he strode out. Due to my own inexperience and relative youth, I puffed up my chest and said, "what did you say?" in my most pompous voice.

Without breaking stride, as he walked by me, he shouted,

"Are you deaf as well as stupid?"

I was so stunned and taken by surprise, that I had to suppress a laugh and carry on with the lesson.

Gripper

My first month of teaching, I encountered Mr Robinson.

Mick Robinson was a history teacher with a bulbous red nose that suggested some long experience of alcohol assimilation over the years. Self-medicating the stress of teaching no doubt.

He had at one time, been in the merchant navy.

His nickname was Gripper. When I innocently asked in the staffroom, how he got his nickname, I was told simply.

"In the days when you could, he did"

Rather alarmed by this revelation I pursued the conversation.

"Er, what do you mean exactly by that?" I asked uneasily.

Way back when corporal punishment was allowed, it seems that if a pupil aggravated him or disrupted the learning of his class, he would get the child loosely round the neck in his 'grip', hence the nickname and pin them to the wall. Often with their little legs and not so little legs, dangling against the wall. He was a big man. After he had proceeded to give them a verbal blast and telling off, but before they started turning blue in the face, he would drop them unceremoniously to the floor. Mostly they landed on their feet. Literally and by chance. Long after corporal punishment was banned, his nickname stayed.

He was an old-style teacher but held in some esteem by former pupils.

Inexplicably he always got the most gifts at the end of the year from students I was told, and more ex-pupils came back to see him than any other teacher!

Make of that what you will.

He retired at the end of my first year in teaching.

In the Beginning

"Oh, wow you'll be treated like a God here".

The first words of the headmistress on the first day of the initial placement on my PGCE post graduate teacher training course in the early 1990s.

I was rather mystified by her comments, in fact completely disconcerted. She explained.

"This is an Infant School, Mr MacDonald, at Greenwood we deal with Reception up to Year 2. So, 4- to 7-year-olds basically. A sad fact is that many of these infants have virtually no male role model in their lives at all! All my teachers are female, despite my best efforts!" she paused in momentary frustration.

"All my support staff are female, my admin staff are female, as are all the kitchen staff. The only permanent male that many of them see is a soon-to-retire Caretaker, Fred, we share with the Junior School next door."

Mrs Pattison was a young Headteacher, at around probably 35, with what sounded like a soft Edinburgh cadence in her voice. Echoes of Miss Jean Brodie I thought, in a rather cliched stereotyped way. Efficient and full of energy, yet warm and very happy in her role evidently. She recommended.

"So that's what I mean, not only are you male, but you're also tall, how tall are you in fact. Not that it matters".

"Er, 6 foot 2", I offered.

She resumed her brief briefing in her office, which lasted about 10 minutes, then she had another urgent meeting on the phone with social services.

Mrs Pattison explained that although the Infant and Junior School were at one time a single creation, they were now run as two separate schools, although, 95% of her infants would go on the short walk to the Junior School next door.

So, she sent me to work with Miss Pretty and with her Year 1 class.

I was at an Infant School in the Welsh borders. The school was in the centre of social housing, with a number of consequent issues. Set against the beautifully peaceful olive green and brown hills of Ruabon Moors beyond the town, it was difficult to believed there would be 'issues'.

Sure enough, when I went into the classroom I was treated as a curiosity by the little infants, if not a God, mercifully.

I could understand why the Junior School children next door called them ankle biters. Because most of the time they did appear to be around my ankles, and I was genuinely frightened of stepping on one of them. Especially as some of the time they were sitting on the floor, principally when they were being read to by the teacher, Miss Pretty. The children clearly adored her.

They had a small square carpet area in the classroom, where they would sit cross legged and chins up to listen to Samantha Pretty reading to them from whatever age-appropriate book they were experiencing at the time.

To explain. This was an obligatory placement for secondary school teacher trainees.

The primary school trainees had to do a similar stint in a secondary school. On my course of about 100 university students, I was the only one to be placed in an Infant School which was relatively close to where I was living at the time. The Junior School next door already had a student teacher placement. First come first served.

Yet, the three weeks went remarkably quickly, which is a sign that I was enjoying my time there and the children were delightful for the most part. As part of my placement, I had to do an extended essay on one of the pupils for my university tutor. I can't remember how many words. These days you'd probably have to ask the parents' permission, but at the time the main class teacher in Year 1 chose the pupil for me.

A boy called Shane.

Every couple of days I would kidnap Shane and take him to the back of the class where we would have a little chat in relative quiet. Surprisingly for a lad brought up in the Welsh borders he was a fan of Leeds United football team. For a 5-year-old he seemed to know a lot about the club he apparently supported. Could be something to do with the fact they were the last team to win the old First Division in England before the advent of the English Premier League. I was amazed at the number of uncles he had. Until it was pointed out to me by an older and cannier teacher that these 'uncles' were just a series of mum's boyfriends during the 5 years since he had been born. Possibly one of them had introduced him to Leeds United?

He was a well looked after and a cheerful young man.

At the end of the three weeks, I had formed a bond naturally with Shane.

He asked me on my final day at Greenwood Infants if I would like to be his uncle. Not even having met his mother, I told him no thank you politely and that I was going to a different school, a long way away. Which I was. He handed me a rather squishy, mildly warped Snickers bar for my journey. Shane had been known to help himself without paying, at the local newsagents. So I left the peanut treat behind with Miss Pretty, just in case.

The 'Bible'

The National Curriculum was set up in the dying days of Mrs Thatcher's government and came into force in 1989. Generally, it was a good idea to standardise the subject content across the country. The country being England and not the rest of the United Kingdom.

However in introducing the National Curriculum (NC), a lot of the advice from teachers and educationalists was ignored in the first instance certainly in the Science National Curriculum of which I should know a fair deal.

When I started my P.G.C.E course in the autumn of 1990 the National Curriculum document, which was a large ring folder with numerous inserts, was akin to the Bible on the course I was doing at a university in the midlands. The P.G.C.E was also one of the first school-based courses in the country, so that after our initial and obligatory three weeks in a primary school placement, we then spent only one day a week in the university and the other four days in a secondary school.

The course tutors had to visit every student teacher on a regular basis, in order to observe lessons and to give detailed feedback and support if necessary.

On one occasion, my tutor Dr Wright, who had a PhD in Microbiology, came into school to meet with me and see me teaching a lesson. This occasion we had chosen a Year 7 class, doing a 3-part lesson on Energy in food.

I invited the class into the lab and asked them to take their seats and get out their equipment, exercise books and so on. The main teacher of the class, Mrs Bailey was sitting in the prep room with the door open, listening as she marked some books. Once they were settled and mostly facing the front, I introduced my tutor.

There was a strange man sitting at the back of the class with a metal clip-board, it would be impolite to pretend he wasn't there!

"We've got a visitor sitting at the back of the room Year 7, Dr Wright, who has come to see your lesson".

At which point I expected to start the lesson. However, at the mention of Dr Wright, about 10 pupils got up and rushed over to him.

"Dr, my tummy hurts"

"Dr, I've got a really bad papercut, look!"

"Dr, do you have any tablets for my hay fever? It's getting bad?"

Sam Wright made sympathetic noises and tried to explain, he wasn't that sort of doctor. The children returned to their seats; a bit confused but placated.

"Er, he's not a medical doctor, Year 7. He's a Doctor of Microbiology." Blank faces looked at me.

"Microbiology, the study of microbes, small living things" I volunteered, keen to get started.

"Is Sean a microbe Sir? He's VERY small." Offered Daizy impishly.

"Mmm no, he's just hasn't had his growth spurt yet" I replied.

Sean had gone bright crimson. This wasn't a promising start.

Feedback point 1. Don't humiliate the pupils!

I always tended to call Year 7 to 9, pupils and Years 10 and above students. It varies from school to school.

The Science National Curriculum started off with 17 Attainment Targets. Yes seventeen.

In each A.T. were numerous bullet points which referred to a particular aspect of that teaching topic. It was a truly enormous document. By and large not only for student teachers, but for qualified teachers in schools, a lot of time was genuinely spent ticking boxes of the hundreds and hundreds of bullet points in the immense Science National Curriculum. I've no idea what other subjects were like, but it was a full-time job and then some, to match every lesson plan to the NC.

Each lesson had to be tailored to a particular Attainment Target and within that, to a particular bullet-pointed sub-level! We didn't know any different being on the teacher training course, but the teachers in schools were totally overwhelmed by the sheer scale of the detail.

The idea was good, but the implementation was not thought through, neither the implications for an actual working school.

I think it was on a Friday when we were all in the uni towards the end of the year long course, that a motorcycle courier turned up at the Education Department of the University and delivered copies of a slimmed down version of the National Curriculum with only 5 Attainment Targets!

An extraordinary moment.

I'm not sure anything was deleted from the original Science N.C. but it was condensed, to use a scientific keyword.

We had spent the best part of a year carrying around this document trying to match lessons and even parts of lessons to a particular bullet point in the National Curriculum and right at the end of the course we were presented with a new version. Ho hum.

I wish I could say this was the end of the Science NC reworking, but not at all. Another version was published to replace the second version. This then more or less continued in place for some years. Thankfully.

In the 'final' version, Attainment Target 2 was effectively Biology, Attainment Target 3, Chemistry and AT4 was Physics. That left Attainment Target 1 for investigative work, or 'practicals' as they are more commonly known by pupils.

The much-used maxim in school Science departments is:

If it's green and wriggles, it's Biology, if it stinks, it's Chemistry and if it doesn't work, it's Physics! There are other renderings of this which are less serviceable in a school!

This final version of 4 A.T.s made a lot more sense, using the traditional divisions of biology, chemistry and physics which had been around for decades. Who knew! Essentially, what Science teachers had been suggesting from the start......

These days, the National Curriculum is hardly ever mentioned in schools and seems to be withering on the vine.

The original NC was set up to provide,

quote: 'a programme of study for children from 5 to 16 in local authority run schools.'

With the advent of the academies programme under New Labour and then continued under the LibDem coalition government and the Conservatives, academies do not have to teach the NC, as they are not local authority run schools.

There are fewer and fewer local authority run schools!

After a very few years the NC has fragmented which is a shame.

Incidentally, having tried to search for National Curriculum on google, (other search engines are available), I find that it is now stored in…

The National Archives.gov.uk.

Hmm. All that work!

Now that most schools are a part of Academy Chains, the NC doesn't have to apply. Clearly examination boards must provide a Specification (Syllabus!) for teaching GCSE and equivalents and A levels and so on.

One might be forgiven for thinking that some interested parties have a lot of shares in publishing companies. Since every change means textbooks and websites must be amended and updated.

The strangest change in recent years has been a reverting of GCSE grades from letters back to a number grading system. So, from A* to G, back to Grades 9 to 1. For the sake of what exactly? Just an extraordinary amount of extra administration for Examination Boards and for schools. Amusingly, one of the major Exam Boards, Edexcel, is owned by Pearson, once owners of the Financial Times and of numerous school textbooks and very fine textbooks indeed.

Sleuthing

I t is often quite useful to have a free period as a teacher in a school and one day I was very glad I had a free. I took a group of Year 9 pupils into an IT suite which I had pre-booked. So that they could do some research for a key practical that we were about to do the following lesson.

It was lesson 1 and the students were slightly comatose but gradually waking up.

I went around the room checking that they all could log on properly and making sure they were not on the omnipresent games.

Very early on, about 5 minutes into the lesson, I noticed that three girls sitting next to each other were unusually giggly for that time in the morning. They were passing around a bottle of water between them and taking sips. This was years before COVID19, so spreading germs was not quite as high on the agenda.

As this bottle was provoking such usual attention, I thought it might be something other than water.

The bottle appeared to be owned by Trixie and I went over to where they were sitting and took the bottle off her. At this point I realised that something unusual was going on. Normally a student would not allow a teacher to take their personal property off them so easily or so readily.

I put the now half empty bottle onto my desk and continued to move around the suite helping individual pupils.

After about 20 minutes, the assistant headteacher, Kay Foster popped her head into the room.

"Is Brandon in today, Sir?" He wasn't.

Just as she was about to leave and continue her rounds of the school, I beckoned to her to wait outside the door so I could have a quick word with her.

I showed her the bottle and told her of my suspicions.

She unscrewed the bottle top and took a sniff over the neck of the bottle.

"Nope, I can't smell anything Sir, you're getting paranoid!"

She went on her way, I put the bottle back on my desk. At the end of the lesson all the pupils saved their work, logged off and got ready for lesson 2. I had been monitoring Trixie as closely as possible out of the corner of my eye and her behaviour was certainly odd, but then again she was a teenager.

As the class left the room, Trixie took her bottle and smiled at me and left for period 2. I still had my suspicions and was still concerned.

Period 2 was a free period, so I looked up Trixie's whereabouts on the school systems and I went to find her in history. I made some excuse with the teacher in the history room and asked to see Trixie outside.

"Trixie, is there anything in that bottle that shouldn't be there?"

"Such as what?" she tried to outstare me.

"Have you put alcohol in that water bottle?"

"No".

I asked for the bottle, and she went into the class and got it for me. I had an idea.

Back in the science prep room, science technicians were busy rushing around getting practicals ready. I found a clean test tube, half filled it with the water from Trixie's bottle. I then went to the chemical store and got some potassium dichromate, which is a brown-yellow liquid. In the presence of alcohol, it turns green.

I put a few drops of the dichromate into the sample of her water, and it went immediately green. Ha!

The Head of Chemistry in the school, Dave Vaskin, knew most information about all things chemical. He had a PhD from Cambridge, but he didn't like using his title as Dr Vaskin. Which was his prerogative. In any case I asked him if anything else could turn the dichromate green.

He looked puzzled but said no that was the standard test for alcohol.

I went back into the prep room and phoned Kay, the assistant head and told her what we had done in Science. There was indeed alcohol in the water bottle.

"Oh, for goodness' sake, really?" she groaned. "OK I'll deal with it right now".

She went back to the history department to find Trixie again and told her what I had done.

Trixie, faced with the clear or rather green, evidence, promptly admitted she had filled about half the bottle with vodka from her dads supply before leaving home in the morning. She obviously knew vodka has little odour.

By now she was looking a bit unsteady on her feet, so we called dad to come and collect her and take her to the local clinic to get checked out. Luckily, she couldn't have sipped too much of the dilute vodka and even more providentially I had a free lesson in order to investigate! The Science department bought me a fancy dress deerstalker and pipe to celebrate!

Threats of Violence

Many people think that threats of violence are something that teachers must deal with regularly, however in my experience they are thankfully very rare. It's the new type of persistent low-level disruption which annoys teachers the most and saps their energy.

"Can I go to the toilet Sir?"

"I don't have a pen, Miss?"

"Why can't I have my bag on the table?"

"Why can't I sit next to Chantelle?"

"Why can't I put my make-up on in the lesson?"

"I was just looking at the time!" (Phone out, yet clock on wall)

Some lessons are endlessly stop start, stop start, stop start, stop start, as the teacher has to deal with relentless low-level interruptions by a minority of pupils who seem to think they are the centre of the universe. All, of course at the expense of the majority of pupils who want to do the right thing and just get on learning.

It's often difficult for the teacher, him or herself, to concentrate on what they need to teach amid the constant interruptions. Especially if the teacher needs to explain a complicated theory or principle. If the teacher labours to concentrate, how much worse must it be for the majority of well-behaved students.

Mind you in terms of violence I have had to break up a couple of fights in classrooms over the years and a few in playgrounds, very rare indeed but nevertheless stressful and difficult. In most cases the students involved are mainly boys, but sometimes girls as well. They are desperate for the teacher to intervene as they are squaring up against each other. The last thing they want to do is fight! They just can't back down. So, they're just looking for the teacher to get in between them and calm things down. Very often the problem will be something that has happened outside of the classroom and usually outside the school. An issue the previous weekend maybe? Which will have been simmering away for hours or days before it explodes in a classroom incident. The teacher blissfully unaware until it explodes. The pupils are usually visibly relieved when a teacher gets between them. It can take a few seconds depending on where they are in the classroom. However, they will continue to try and get at each other physically for a bit to save face. I got my arm strained at one time separating two 6-foot Year 11 boys who happened to be on the rugby team.

In terms of direct threats to me, again very rare indeed. Overall if a student was becoming aggressive, I would tend to move towards them in a calm and measured manner, rather than away from them. Backing away, doesn't look good and often has a counterproductive effect.

More petite women teachers are often safer than large, tall male teachers, because a pupil would have zero credibility and zero kudos with his mates for attacking a small female teacher. However, he might get more kudos for decking a male teacher!

Thankfully, that never happened to me, and I can't remember it happening in any school I've been in, despite the fact that I have been in some challenging schools! Challenging schools is the usual term for difficult schools with a difficult intake. Or possibly an average intake, with very ineffective management at the top wedded to ideology rather than school performance.

The only time I can remember being definitely frightened, was at a school in the summer term when we as senior managers we were rounding up the children who were sitting on the grass, to get them to go back into lessons for the afternoon after lunchtime.

Some groups were obviously more truculent than others. I found myself one day herding in the stragglers from the school field and chivvying them back into the buildings, when I noticed I was on my own with two girls.

Aimey and Kaycee, two Year 10 students. One of them started to become verbally aggressive. Shouting at me

"I'm gonna punch you in the face Sir,"

"I'm gonna take your glasses and smash them Sir."

"What are you gonna to do about it if I did Sir?"

Interesting she ended each threat with a Sir?

The most frightening part of this, was not the verbal aggression or even direct threats, it was the realisation that I was out of the sight of the CCTV cameras placed around the outside of the school buildings. I started to walk faster all the while pretending to ignore these threats and making a beeline for an area on the way into the building, where I knew a CCTV camera was trained. I wasn't frightened of being punched in the face or any other physical violence. I was frightened of having to restrain this teenage girl without any witnesses, apart from the one other girl accompanying us, as we were strutting rapidly back into school. The other female student to her credit remained silent and looked rather embarrassed. However, could I rely on her as an accurate witness if I had to restrain the first girl, Aimey? Fortunately, as we walked faster and faster towards the buildings, I was aware that we were finally in line of sight of a CCTV camera. Which I knew was working as we had used it earlier in the day to investigate a report someone was seen on the school grounds the previous night around 10pm. It was digitally recording. At this point my relief must been obvious and Aimey was also probably aware that she was now on camera, although I didn't mention it. She began to calm down and soon we were back in the corridor where I ushered them back into their respective classes before I went to my own. That was just bad luck. But I really should have kept an eye on the situation with the other senior staff, so I didn't get isolated as I did.

In any case the matter resolved itself quickly. I went to my class and began the last lesson of the day, rather shaken up and humbled by my own folly at finding myself in that situation. I think that is one reason teaching is so stressful. You cannot relax too much, at any time.

Sometimes there is a push to perhaps have cameras in all classrooms, but there is understandably some reluctance to go down this route. A bit Big Brother?

The teaching unions would be wary. I think I would be quite happy to be teaching in a classroom with a live camera. There are of course legal implications. I can see both signs of the argument.

The same girl, Aimey, caused a similar grief to me a few months later but for very different reasons. There was a free bus service running between the two sites of this split site school. The Years 7 to 9 on one site and the Years 10 and 11 students on the other. Double decker buses would run between sites before school and after school. On one occasion it was reported to me that Aimey had been extremely offensive and used foul and obscene language on the bus one day to the driver, going from the upper site to the lower school site. I found her and told her she would have to find alternative arrangements to get back home the next day. She wasn't happy. I told Aimey that she was aware of the rules for using the transport to and from school and so were her parents when they signed the home-school contract. These two sites were only about a mile apart, maybe a mile and a half at most. I tried calling her parents earlier in the day on both the landline and mobile with no luck.

However as we were boarding the buses, on which there were always two teachers for each journey, she came up to me with a mobile phone and shoved it in my face saying.

"Sir, my mum wants to speak to you. I took the phone rather apprehensively from Aimey and politely asked who I was speaking to.

The conversation, if that is what it can be described as, was brief but to the point and is just burned on my mind.

"Oi, what's this about you not letting Aimey on the bus back home?"

I started to explain the situation…….the mum cut over me and said and I quote word for word as I wrote it down 10 minutes later,

"If you don't f****** let my daughter on the bus right f****** now, I will come up to that school, put my fist down your throat and pull your f****** heart out".

I replied that Aimey wouldn't be getting the bus and that I would probably be at the school until 6:00 pm and I would be delighted to speak to her when she came up to the school. At which point she slammed the phone down or whatever the equivalent is with a mobile. It did sound as though the phone might have hit a wall....

Aimey managed to get a lift back home with a mum of a friend. The staff overseeing the bus boarding went back into the school and I got on with some work in my classroom, fully expecting the mother to come up and see me. I had plenty of work to do anyway, however by 18:00 hours she hadn't appeared strangely, and I left the school and drove home. We heard no more from mum, although the Headteacher asked me to record the conversation in writing and we had no further problems with Aimey abusing staff or other students on the school buses.

In all truthfulness, what is often described as good behaviour in schools is often barely acceptable. We have all become used to a lower standard of behaviour.

It's interesting to see that Ms Katharine Birbalsingh at the Michaela Community School in Wembley, seems to have managed to create a very disciplined environment in a school that has numerous ethnicities and social poverty. I have not visited the school but I know a few who have done so. Every account I have received indicates that the students there are very happy and very relaxed. They know they can learn without distractions. Ms Birbalsingh was apparently a member of the Socialists Workers Party at Oxford.

She made the mistake of speaking at a Conservative Party Conference, although not being a member of the Conservative Party. That simple speech has meant she is still regarded with suspicion by many in teaching. I'm sure that it doesn't matter where the educational theories come from............ if it works, it works!

Protecting Pupils from Themselves and Others

O ccasionally it's necessary to intervene between pupils to protect them or to protect other pupils and very, very occasionally a teacher or other member of staff. In my second year of teaching, I was on lunchtime playground duty for the last 10 minutes and I heard the familiar sounds of "Fight! Fight! Fight! etc as pupils began to crowd around something taking place.

A Year 7 boy called Corey had clearly lost the plot for whatever reason, the red mist had descended and he was on top of another Year 7 boy Matthew. Both boys were more or less the same size, but the clear difference was that Corey was out of control entirely. He began slamming Matthew's head against the concrete paving surface of the playground.

Corey was insensible to the fact that there was anyone else in the vicinity. He was in his own world, intent on a reckoning. I was desperately hoping a more experienced teacher would be nearer to break this up, but no one appeared, and I couldn't wait for even a few seconds or Matthew's skull would have been fractured on the unforgiving surface.

I managed to grab Corey round the chest, and I literally had to pull him off Matthew. Thankfully I was strong enough to pull him away. I'm not sure a petite woman teacher would have been. A few of the older boys seeing that

I was struggling, assisted me in restraining and calming him at least, and very quickly other teachers arrived including the Head of Year 7 who started to disperse the crowd of excitable pupils, once she saw that the two boys had been safely detached from each other.

The Head of Year, Mrs Wimpole took the two boys away and Matthew was taken to hospital as a precaution, for his skull to be checked.

It's always difficult knowing when to intervene and when not to intervene, but in this case it really was a matter of urgency. Without an intervention, it could have been literally life threatening for Matthew. No doubt Matthew had been provoking Corey and winding him up, but that was for the Head of Year to investigate. Laying hands on pupils is always risky for teachers and that is why it is very rarely done. That is also the reason teachers have unions with legal teams in the background.

5 minutes later it was the end of lunchtime and the classes started to line up for their various departments and lessons, still buzzing with some fever about the sudden violence they had witnessed. I went straight to teach my science lesson but was anxiously thinking about what I had done and hoping Matthew was OK.

After school, as we were having a coffee in the science prep room, other members of staff were congratulating me on acting so swiftly. Being inexperienced, I was still unsure. Remarkably, David, another science teacher who lives very close to the school, told us that when Corey was in primary school, he had climbed up onto the roof of the local pub which his dad either managed or owned and remained there for three hours until the police came to talk him down. A road having to be closed off in the process.

Corey had a history of let's say extreme behaviour.

A few months later I was complaining to the deputy headteacher, Mr Singh about the off the wall behaviour of one or two pupils, as we met in the corridor after school.

His answer stuck with me for many years. He said,

"Mark, you know all the adults who end up in mental hospitals; well, they were children once" and then he slowly walked away.

It's true to say, that in some cases, we assume that mental health problems begin on a person's 18th birthday, when in reality there is no cut off point at which an individual child becomes an individual adult. Well, there is legally, but certainly not developmentally.

There is of course Child and Adolescent Mental Health Services, CAMHS, but inevitably they are overstretched and with long waiting lists. It cannot just be a matter of funding and money. Somehow local communities and extended families need to step up and offer support to troubled children.

Very easy to say I know, how much harder to do!

Labour Exchange

The birth of our first daughter was scheduled to take place in a large local teaching hospital, not too far from the school I was working in at the time. My wife, Dew, went into labour at about 5.15pm and we went to the hospital as instructed.

A chilly day in March turned into an even colder March evening and night. The ice glistening on the roads and pavements looking more like a glassy speckled surface with every passing minute. Reflecting the red car brake lights and orange streetlights like a shifting mirror orb.

Dew's waters broke in an avalanche of amniotic fluid onto the floor of the reception ward, and she was quickly put into a wheelchair and taken up to the delivery suite. I followed dutifully, carrying the bags. We were put into the delivery room and settled down for the big event. Lots of squeezing hands and visits from doctors and midwives as well as a trainee midwife, Zoe, quite a young woman who was obviously already a qualified nurse, but now training to step up to midwifery. She was not directly responsible for anything other than her own training experience, so she was allowed to flip between various delivery rooms to gain maximum experience in the different stages of labour. Dew's labour was relatively quick at around 2 hours and a beautiful healthy baby girl was announced to the world on St Patrick's Day.

This was in the late 90s, I don't think we had a mobile phone at the time, so I was dispatched to inform her mother, who was at home in the flat and to my parents up in North Wales about the new addition to the family. I remember using a payphone in the hospital. A momentous occasion for the family as this was the first grandchild for both sides of the family. Returning back up to the delivery room with a paper cup of hot chocolate for my wife, I passed a lady who looked familiar, I knew I had met her somewhere, but I really wasn't sure where. A realisation gradually materialised in my mind as I was comforting my wife on her painful but successful delivery.

Could the lady I passed in the corridor be one of the parents I had met during a parents evening? Surely not. I slowly realised she was the mother of Lauren, a Year 11 girl I taught. I thought she had recognised me as I had her, but she had seemed reluctant to acknowledge me for some reason as we passed in the hospital passage.

I remembered she had an older daughter who must have given or be giving birth in the very next delivery room!

When Zoe came back into our suite, I heard her talking to one of the nurses about a Lauren who had also just given birth to a baby girl.

It hit me suddenly that Lauren was my Year 11 pupil, who I remembered had been absent from school for some weeks. Not yet 16 but already a mother.

It does happen from time to time that a girl gets pregnant, the youngest I remember was in Year 8, but usually it is kept on a need-to-know basis in a school.

If you are too far down the pecking order, you don't need to know! Which is fair enough. It's a highly delicate topic. The more people that know means more impending and harmful gossip.

For a school, if they shower an underage pregnant pupil with too much special consideration, it can look to her peers as if it's a jolly good idea to get pregnant. If only for the extra attention it gets. A frustrating balancing act for the school and its management and pastoral team.

Usually, it is kept quiet within the school for that reason and a girl just stays at home with the local education authority providing home tuition. Not ideal. It's not an ideal situation but it has to be somehow managed.

Marie and the Atmosphere

In my first few years of teaching, it wasn't unusual to have a very unbalanced gender ratio in a class, especially at the upper age level. I was never entirely clear as to why this should be the case. It has something to do with the fact that the school had been a split site school and moved onto one site and some of the parents didn't like their daughters going to the new site.

On one Friday morning I had a Year 11 class who were unusually subdued, I couldn't really work out why. Was it due to my lack of experience? In any case I thought I would make the most of it and try tackling a slightly harder topic in chemistry. We started looking at covalent bonds. The lads were quiet and attentive, when it suddenly dawned on me that it was an entirely male class. For some reason this set had been formed using their Sats results from Year 9 and I ended up having 22 boys and 3 girls in this set. It hadn't really occurred to me previously that this was particularly unusual, but on this one day, all three girls were either absent or really very late to school. It was still lesson 1.

We were looking at atomic structure and I was then going to look at chemical bonds. This was not a top group and I was expecting a bit of resistance, yet the boys were on task and completely focused. Well, OK not completely focused but pretty much as good as it gets on a Friday with a middle ability group.

"It can't be surely?" I pondered as I was going through these chemistry dynamics.

"Could it be the absence of girls, that was causing the renewed and unusual attention?" I dismissed it as being fanciful.

As my classroom faced into one of the playgrounds, I could see across the whole playground towards the entrance foyer of the school, I noticed one of the three absent girls leave the foyer and cross the playground heading towards my lab.

Marie was at least 20 minutes late to the lesson, on top of missing the morning registration. So very late indeed, even for her. I continued teaching the class all the while watching Marie's slow progress trundling across the playground. Well, this is a science lab I thought, what better place to have my own psychological prediction. Would Marie's entry to the classroom make any difference to the atmosphere? We would soon find out. She entered the classroom and as it happened was sitting in the second row back on the left not far from the door. No apology was forthcoming for her tardiness from Marie, so I ignored it and made a mental note to speak to her at the end. She sat down and took her coat and bag off.

Within two or three minutes of her coming into the classroom, the atmosphere did indeed change and the boys were getting more restless. I changed the type of activity and still there was a notable change in the atmosphere. Many of the boys who had been quiet and attentive started showing off and calling out.

It really wasn't my imagination! Even allowing for my own unconscious bias towards the situation, the boys were becoming more difficult to keep on task and towards the end of the lesson it was becoming more fraught. There was absolutely no reference to Marie, at least not one I heard, and she didn't speak to anyone else. Clearly this wasn't her fault in any way, yet simply her presence had provoked an increase in attention seeking behaviour, more challenges directed to me and generally a less studious atmosphere. I began to wish I hadn't started on this topic anyway.

At morning breaktime, I mentioned this to the other science teachers and technicians in the science prep room, and one of my colleagues a Welshman named Ellis listened carefully and then promptly said

"See it's the Peacock effect isn't it. The boys have got no one to show off to when they're on their own and yet assuming most of them are straight, as soon as a young female comes into their vicinity, they start *peacocking*, showing off and the like, you know what I mean".

I did know what he meant because I just witnessed it earlier in the morning and if I hadn't seen it with my own eyes, I wouldn't have believed it!

It really seemed tangible to me.

As we talked a little more over break about the pros and cons of single sex education, I seem to remember some mention of this Peacock effect in my teacher training year at university. I think, at the time, I just dismissed it as probably educational gobbledegook. This whole subject fascinated me, and I asked around. Apparently, there was a school in Essex called Shenfield School which specifically addresses this problem in a mixed school. It was first and foremost a mixed school but the boys and the girls were taught separately for the three core subjects, English Maths and Science in single sex groups. In all the other subjects as well as their pastoral form time, they were in mixed gender groups. This was back in the mid-1990s and I have no idea if this school still continues with this philosophy.

This was long before websites were common and so I got hold of the schools prospectus and sure enough there was a section on the so-called Peacock effect. It was a thing!

I happened to come across this again a few years later when I worked in a boys' state school. It had a wide catchment area and not a particularly academic intake and yes it was probably the easiest school I've ever taught in.

The boys are much more focused. Time and time again I found that if boys had an argument about something even very rarely leading to fisticuffs, it was usually forgotten, done and dusted, the following day.

I found the same with telling boys off or sanctioning them. They just seem to bounce back so much more easily. The following day there was no awkwardness no sulkiness, it was if the previous day hadn't even happened! I really don't know if this single sex teaching in mixed schools is going on anywhere else in the country, it probably is, and it really needs to be looked at in detail. The problem is, as always in education, if it's not flavour of the month or in phase with the current zeitgeist then it just won't be taken seriously.

Shortcuts to Success

During my first couple of years of teaching I learned a very valuable lesson from a more experienced teacher in my Science Department. On the other hand, I was always rather conflicted by his methods!

Do the ends always justify the means?

Kevin Clarke was a good teacher from Scotland. However, he was also a lazy teacher at times and would usually take a shortcut if he could possibly do so. At the end of the first year of teaching and at the very end of term, when the timetables were published for the following September, each teacher found out which classes they were going to take-over. I was interested to see who would be taking over my very difficult 8F Science class, who had been the most taxing and challenging of my first year.

I was surprised when Kevin Clarke came to see me during the last week of the summer term. We both had a free period at the same time coincidentally and things were a bit quieter now that the Year 11 students were on study leave and in fact most had already finished their GCSE and equivalents by July.

The sun was radiating through the classroom windows when he walked in, apparently casually, just to have a chat. Mr Clarke had a reputation as a bit of a gossip. So, I was wary as to what I should say or could say. This was a time in the early 90s when smoking had not been banned in public places and schools normally had a smokers room for teachers and other staff to go to smoke. Inevitably it was the same teachers and staff who congregated and inevitably there was a fair amount of gossip in the smokers group. As Mr. Clarke was a smoker I was even more wary.

He told me that he was taking over my difficult Year 8 Science group 8F into 9F, as they would be in September. There were occasionally a couple of students moved in and out of a class set, but generally it was the same class handed over to the subsequent teacher in the new academic year.

"I will be taking 8F into 9F in September, so I see".

He began on what I promptly realised was a bit of a fishing expedition.

"I know that they were a pretty difficult class for you?" stating the obvious, as we had all been in the same monthly departmental meetings when we discussed classes and pupils.

I agreed that they were the most challenging class that I had encountered that year. He then asked me a question a bit out of left field which I was not expecting.

"Now which would you say was your best pupil then, the one who never put a foot wrong, a model pupil if you like. One that you'd like to adopt yourself?"

This was a bit of a running joke at parents' evenings when if you were speaking to the parents of a particularly good polite, well-mannered and hard-working pupil, you might tell the parents.

"Would you mind if I adopted young Sean" or whatever the name happened to be. This usually pleased the parents immensely, clearly they were proud to hear a teacher, if only in jest, ask if they could adopt their child!

Yet still I was a bit confused as to why he was asking me who was the best model pupil in the class, normally a teacher would ask who the problem students were, thus getting a heads-up for the following academic year. I didn't need to hesitate an answer.

"Oh, that'll be Abbie, without a doubt, she's a really good pupil in every aspect, always does homework, very cooperative and polite, a complete joy to teach and have in the class."

"Fine now that's interesting" he exclaimed still in a casual manner, as if it wasn't very important and then we had a bit of a chat about what we may be doing over the summer holidays. He was going back to his family in Scotland with his wife and then I think they were off to Greece.

After a while, he left my classroom, probably to go to the smokers' room or maybe back to his own classroom just finish up some loose ends.

I didn't really think anything of it for the rest of that week and then it was the summer holidays. We had a staff BBQ in the quadrangle immediately after the students were dismissed on the last day.

September came round and I returned from a long trip through France with some friends and before long it was the two inset days or teacher training days, at the beginning of September, before the youngsters came back in full force themselves.

Accordingly, we started with our new timetables and the term started to grind into gear. It was still hot in September, in fact hotter than it had been in July and so we suffered a little bit in the heat.

I later found out from a reliable pupil in 8F, now in 9F, what happened in the first lesson with Mr. Clarke. First impressions count! Hence from what I can gather, the lesson started as normal, then about 10 minutes into the lesson Mr. Clarke saw that the model pupil, Abbie, had turned around for a second to look out of the window. This was his moment to pounce. He launched into a tirade of invective towards Abbie, telling her in no uncertain terms to pay attention to him and not turn around. There was some shouting from him, and Abbie was suitably chastised and on the verge of tears.

Now he had the whole classes attention, they were also well aware that Abbie was the perfect pupil and sidelong looks between pupils made it clear what most of them were thinking.

Blimey! if he goes at Abbie like that what's he gonna do with us!

The class were on tenterhooks for the rest of the lesson waiting for another explosion from Mr. Clarke. However, none was needed. He had made his point and how. He completed whatever he had to do on his Lesson Plan. He then dismissed the class keeping Abbie back for a couple of minutes with a friend of hers. He sought to made it right with her and apologised for shouting at her, but pointing out he was just setting out his standards for the year.

I can tell you that the class, 9F, in science, had a much better experience and very much greater learning over the course of that academic year than they had the previous year.

Does the end justify the means?

Many people will feel that it was quite brutal, for Abbie especially. Yet she will have had a much quieter, focused class to work in from the September to the following July, without a shadow of a doubt. Abbie would benefit most from Mr Clarke's cunning! Not to mention his own wish for a quieter life.

The last I heard Mr Clarke and his wife, who was also a teacher at another school, had taken jobs in Lima Peru, teaching in an upmarket private school.

Doing the Splits

This was the first school I had worked in, after I finished my PGCE and because there was a shortage of teachers, as always, especially science teachers, I was able to start in the July, effectively the same month I finished my course. This was to give a clear incentive to new teachers to join a school and start as soon as possible, as they would then be paid for the summer holidays. I was working in a school in a Birmingham borough on a split site which would not be the last time I experienced working on a split site, in this case over 3 miles apart.

Split site schools are not uncommon. On occasions a teacher would have to finish his or her second lesson/period at 11:00 o'clock and rush to their car with any books and other resources they needed, hopefully not dropping anything on the way, through the carpark and then drive through that part of Birmingham, as I said 3 miles, to hopefully arrive at the second site in time to start the lesson at 11:20 am.

No time for a drink, or snack or even going to the toilet. Teachers inevitably often arrived slightly late due to the traffic, and I would find, as I arrived flustered, at the classroom door a group of Year 10 students waiting to be let in and winding each other up in the corridor. Often a deputy headteacher would be waiting in the corridor with a raised eyebrow wondering why I couldn't get there on time, even though he knew full well.

I don't remember him actually tapping his wristwatch, but he did everything but tell me I was late. Due to my naivety and my lack of experience I somehow managed to put up with this nonsense for a whole year before the split size school moved onto a single site. One of the many rules we were taught at the teacher training university, was always arrive at your lesson before the pupils! If you don't, you are forever trying to maintain order unless it is a particularly pliable class. In this school that was impossible. Even allowing for traffic being light and the traffic lights being green, green, green, it was nigh on impossible to arrive on time. A fact that the deputy head teacher who was a maths teacher was bizarrely unable to understand. Growl.

I should never ever, ever, have put up with this torture. That is the advantage of having teaching unions. Some unions are more moderate than others. Some members want to merge all teaching unions to form a super union. I prefer choice. However, at this stage I didn't know any better.

After a couple of years, I was promoted to assistant Head of Year so was required to attend the school pastoral meetings at which the Headteacher was present. There was at this time a governmental push for healthy eating in schools which of course we had included in the PHSE programme. Some schools call this Citizenship. However, the school at the same time placed strategically, in various corridors of the school vending machines selling chocolate bars and fizzy drinks, crisps and so on. This was a good source of revenue for the school apparently.

At one of the pastoral meetings, I did bring up this contradiction between teaching healthy eating whilst at the same time, selling unhealthy options in the vending machines. This was noted in the minutes of the meeting. The next day I got called to the Head's office and he told me in no uncertain terms that he was not best pleased.

Ideals come up against reality.

Unpredictable Outcomes

As with many schools, there is usually a trip for each year group at the end of the summer term. It's a good bonding exercise and can be educational in all sorts of ways, even for the teaching staff.

Going ice skating at a local rink for example or to the Theatre in London or to a theme park. It's also a hold that Heads of Year can use over their charges.

"If I hear of one more incident like that, you won't be going on the end of year trip, young man/young lady." Delete as appropriate.

This particular year our Year 10 group had drawn the best adventure and we were going to a theme park in the South of England. Many people expect this to be a bit of a jolly for the teachers, but as ever, with children of whatever age it is difficult to relax completely.

Even with one's own children you have to be alert, as all parents know!

When it is other peoples' children, in bulk, you really need eyes everywhere. The only possible downside to a theme park trip is the British weather. These trips must be booked months in advance usually for maybe 150 students, as do the coaches and any necessary cover needed in the school. It's almost impossible to change the dates as there will be literally hundreds if not thousands of schools looking for dates around the same time.

Last time I went we were very lucky with the weather. It was a warm sunny day but not oppressively hot or dangerously sunny. Win, win. Looking at the weather forecast we could see a pretty accurate view of the day, so the students were well prepared with drinking water. It's not possible to go around a theme park in a group of around 150 students, whether they are 11- or 15-year-olds. Once we got on the coaches, we reiterated very simple rules that they must not in any circumstances go round the park on their own. Preferably they should be in groups of three or four, but the minimum was with one other student, at all times. This usually works well and it's an enjoyable day. Lots of screaming and laughing and usually no incidents at all. I was acting as form tutor on this day and the Head of Year was Elena Carter who was known to be strict but fair with her Year 10 cohort. As this was July, they were about to go into Year 11 in September, and she needed to keep them on a tight rein for the last year.

Having been to theme parks in the USA, one weird thing I noticed was that all the theme parks in the States that we visited with our children, had spotlessly clean toilets with no malodour at all. The same could not be said of British theme parks. Usually, the toilets were hygienic and clean and yet there was a certain odour which didn't seem to be present in the US. Absolutely no smoking is allowed in US theme parks as far as I could see, and no other unpleasantness was allowed either!

On this particular day we were rounding the teens up to get back to the coach park and head back to school for the parents to collect. The teachers were checking-in their own classes on a written register quite close to the park exit and not far from a large toilet block.

It was as we were checking off our own form groups that a man in his early 30s came up to us looking extremely embarrassed. He asked which one of us was in charge of the whole group and we all pointed to Elena who was standing a few metres away, watching as the students arrived back at the rendezvous point. Counting them out and counting them in, is a fairly simple process, but you never can tell.

I do remember a previous school ski trip went to Austria during the Easter holidays with 40 children. One of them got left up a mountain as the rest headed back to the hotel. Hard to believe but it did happen. Luckily there were no catastrophic outcomes, but the party leader got a rollicking back in the UK.

Anyway, the man in his 30s walked over to Elena still looking very disconcerted. He told her that one of our young ladies, 15 years old remember, was going up to random men as they were going in and out of the male toilets and telling them she would have sex for £20 behind the toilet block! Lots of the men coming out of the toilet block were walking very quickly away from the area and all credit to the one man who reported the matter. There were understandably no takers, but you never can tell what teenagers are going to do. We got them all back on the coaches and back to school and clearly the young lady was referred for support.

You really can't relax, let alone predict what may or may not happen on a school trip!

Perry Benton

"**G**ive me strength"

Perry was a boy invariably in trouble throughout Year 8 and the Head of Year 8 could often be heard muttering her usual aside in the staff room, *give me strength!*

Mrs Doubleday was a no-nonsense IT teacher and Head of his Year, with a soft Suffolk accent and plenty of patience, but with very clear expectations. Perry was a student who would try the patience of a saint. Another of Mrs Doubleday's favourite sayings!

This time Perry had accomplished a particularly difficult week and came to the attention of Mrs Doubleday on numerous occasions. Not least because of his liberal use of bad language, including the F word. Especially so for a 12-year-old boy. His most stand out moment during the week nevertheless was to somehow get into the staff car park and creep around to such an extent for 10 minutes, that he let down the tyres on at least four separate cars, three teachers and unluckily for him, the headteacher's PA, Miss Mouner.

Perry's dad had a second-hand car business about two miles from the school, maybe he practised his tyre busting skills in his dad's car lot.

By the end of the week Mrs Doubleday had had enough, she rang Perry's father and asked him to come into school to speak to her and the headteacher. Perry had already been suspended for one day on the Wednesday for the tyre incident.

I walked across to the school entrance area immediately after the last lesson to have a meeting with Mr Benton, the headteacher Mr Hall and Mrs Doubleday as I was Perry's form teacher. The normal process would be to have a sit-down meeting in the small glass-sided, purpose-built meeting room which looked out over the foyer.

A short meeting, I hoped.

However, on this occasion we didn't get that far. I found Mr Benton already standing agitatedly in the foyer waiting for us, as the students streamed out of the building for the final time that week. It was Friday afternoon. Mr Benton was a tall well-built man. Perry had clearly not reached his growth spurt yet, as he was probably half the height of his father.

"Look I appreciate Perry is a bit of a handful. I'm looking after him on my own," began his dad, as the Headteacher arrived and started to gently direct Mr Benton into the meeting room. This would be their second meeting of the week as Mr Hall had already spoken to his dad on Perry's 're-entry' after his one-day exclusion.

Mr Benton was not in the mood for a sit-down anything.

By this time, Perry had arrived and stood meekly by his father's side looking at us all apprehensively. So, all five of us remained standing as the pupils continued to file past us, now in decreasing numbers as a school emptied.

"Look Mr Hall, I'm really busy, I've gotta get back to my business aaaasap" he emphasised the sap. "I thought we'd already dealt with this tyre incident. Yeah, he was bang out of order and I've grounded him for the weekend starting right now" He glared at Perry. "Right now."

Mrs Doubleday intervened,

"I'm afraid Mr Benton, on top of that serious incident of damage or damages, I've had numerous reports from various subjects that Perry's language is really and truly awful and unacceptable and he's not even left Year 8 yet!"

Mr Benton was clearly agitated and not in the mood to have a long discussion.

"I'm sorry about that, it won't happen again." Turning to Perry he said.

"Look what have I told you before, you are not to f*****g swear at the f*****g teachers or else you'll have me to f*****g answer to….understand? He spoke with no hint of irony.

He continued.

"Right when we get home, I'm washin your mouth out with washin up liquid, with" he hesitated …"the dishpan brush."

Perry looked alarmed and doubtful at the same time.

Mrs Doubleday was probably torn between wondering if she should contact social services after the weekend and thinking that was exactly what her Ma would have done to her back in Suffolk, if she had been caught using foul language.

This was one of the problems dealing with a minority of parents, they swung wildly from one extreme to the other. Mrs Doubleday had enough, it was the end of a long week, and she held her finger and thumb up to her forehead trying to smooth the lines in her skin and said

"OK well we'll see if there's an improvement next week, but there shouldn't be any need for washing up liquid. Clearly, she could feel an extra report about to land on her shoulders, over a child protection issue! Mr Hall, Mrs Doubleday and I couldn't help exchange a brief amused and bemused look, as we all regarded Mr Benton's apparent lack of awareness of his own use of bad language.

On the other hand maybe he didn't, and it was a clever ploy to bring the stand-up meeting to an end swiftly. He was a second-hand car dealer and no doubt used to thinking on his feet.

It was a Friday evening after all.

As we watched Mr Benton retreating out of school with Perry at his side, all three of us shook our heads, gently shrugged our shoulders slightly and went back to our various rooms to tie up the loose ends before the weekend.

I imagine, on Monday morning one of Mrs Doubledays first jobs when she had a break between teaching, was to have a discussion with social services. One of many.

I eventually left school about 5.45 pm, taking a heavy bag of books to mark at home. As I passed the local Burger King restaurant and DIY warehouse on my drive home, I saw Perry riding his bike, with two other boys, on the pavement of course. So much for him being grounded, or perhaps he had been sent on an errand to buy some washing up liquid. Somehow, I didn't think so.

Two Speeds

"**S**he's got two speeds Mr MacDonald. Slow and dead slow."

Mr Jacobs was explaining his daughter to me as he sat next to his wife at Year 9 parents evening. He thought it would not be a good idea to take Chloe on the field trip to Wales.

I had been asked to lead a joint biology and geography field trip for four days. It was going to take a good deal of planning and organisation, but I was fairly new to teaching, about five years in and I was flattered to be asked to lead the trip. Obviously, I would have other teachers with me. Three of us in total. Plus, the permanent resident staff at the field centre.

I was delighted that Chloe had signed up to come on the trip although a little bit surprised, as she hadn't seemed overly enthused by biology or indeed according to her geography teacher, by geography either. The field trip was to take place in a local authority field centre called I think, Ty Gwyrdd or Green House. It was equipped with classrooms, dining room and dormitories. As well as outdoor expert teachers to accompany us on our mini expeditions. In truth all no more than 20 miles from the field centre! These were Year 9 students and we had fourteen of them in total. 7 boys and 7 girls.

Mr Jacobs was a very affable, congenial and cooperative parent, but I could see that neither he nor his wife thought that Chloe would enjoy the field trip.

She just isn't the field trip type Mr MacDonald. Quite frankly we think she signed up because she's got a crush on you!

I nearly sprayed them with the lukewarm tea I was sipping during the three-hour parents evening. That was something I hadn't expected or foreseen.

Both Mr and Mrs Jacobs looked at me with amused grins and I certainly felt that they probably had a good point in saying that Chloe shouldn't join us on the field trip.

"Well okay, that's something I didn't expect". I spluttered, "if you think you can persuade Chloe to remove herself from the list that might be a good idea."

Mr Jacobs rang me a few days later, only one week before our planned visit to Wales.

"I really sorry Mr MacDonald she's adamant that she wants to go on the field trip, and we can't persuade her otherwise".

This was going to be tricky, but we had signed up 14 students, we decided to go ahead.

I told the Headteacher what Mr Jacobs had said.

She took my hand and shook it tellingly,

"Good luck!" was her only advice. She'd seen it all before.

We had two women teachers with us and one of the permanent staff at the field centre was also female. So, I imagined I'd be able to keep out of Chloe's way.

After a long coach journey, we arrived at Ty Gwyrdd for a beautiful sunny evening as the sun set in the west and after supper everyone went to bed. Boys and girls separately in their own dormitories.

I thought the students would be tired after the long coach journey and I certainly was, as I was in the single room next to the boys dormitory, I could hear them talking, shrieking and being a pain until nearly two am and that was after I had been in several times to warn them to settle down and go to sleep.

The following morning, Trudy the female teacher and Year 9 tutor told me that the girls were much the same and didn't get to sleep until about the same time.

Note to self. Don't let pupils fall asleep on the coach!

So, we left after breakfast in the centre minibus and headed up into the hills. We were going to do a transect sampling of different plant species on the moor and then the following day was going to be devoted to geography.

The weather was good and with a pleasant breeze. The moor was particularly boggy, with lots of tiny brooks and streams weaving in and around the area through the undergrowth, so that we had to tread very carefully.. The field centre had equipped us with proper walking boots, waterproofs and so on. We found a reasonable place to start sampling and the group split up into pairs with the string and posts to start identifying the plants. We needed to get some numerical data on the abundance of plant life in the area so we could use the data back in the classrooms.

After about 45 minutes we were all going great guns and I had all 14 pupils in my line of sight all the time, as I kept looking up. Suddenly there was a scream and I realised I could only count 13 students. Riley had slipped and fallen into a marshy bog and his partner Chloe was shouting for help.

I ran over and Riley had fallen face down into the most foul-smelling muddy bog water. The slimy mud was stagnant and as black as treacle and almost as viscous. Now it had been disturbed by a face-planting Year 9 boy and even stronger odours were emanating from the watery concoction. I really didn't want to get my feet wet as we still had another 4 hours outside in the open. He had now turned his face towards me, and I could see he was unharmed as far as I could tell so I manoeuvred my feet into a relatively dry area and stooped down to pick him out of the bog. Unfortunately, he was heavier than I expected and I slipped. I did my best effort not to fall on top of him. I managed to pivot to avoid him but landed squarely on my back in the same disgusting boggy mass. Each disturbance of the black glutinous water appeared to release more obnoxious odours.

I managed to push him out of the bog as other students pulled him from the drier mounds. He was absolutely soaked and coated in part of Wales.

We couldn't leave him in the open so one of the field trip staff offered to take him back down to the centre and hose him down. Or at least send him off for a shower and try and salvage his clothes. They would have to be sluiced before they could possibly go anywhere near a washing machine!

As I was leading the group, I had no choice but to continue squelching around as we continued our investigations and eventually we sat down for a rest and our packed lunches.

There seemed to be an invisible ring around me for whatever reason. No-one wanted to eat their lunch next to that bouquet.

After 20 minutes or so we continued, using our maps, to a slightly different terrain to do some quadrat surveys. This took us most of the afternoon, then we headed back down to the vehicle. I tried to wipe off as much of the offensive odorous mud from myself and my clothes, but still it was radiating from me in a notably pungent manner.

The driver who had come to pick us up in the minibus, had obviously been forewarned about my state and with some razzing he had set up a seat at the back of the minibus covered in black bin bags to protect the upholstery.

Apparently, this was not an unusual occurrence. My humiliation was complete.

The following days proceeded with no more remarkable incidents as we completed the assignments the school had given us.

When we got back to the school at the end of the fourth day, we managed to arrive more or less at our expected time and all the parents were there to greet the youngsters holding their washing and imparting various anecdotes.

Chloe had clearly had her bubble burst and had spent most of the trip glowering and murmuring, if not in a downright sullen sulk. She was not cut out for the great alfresco.

Her parents were right.

Her dad came up to me as her mum put Chloe's things in the boot and she got into their car. He slapped me on the back. "Thank you for bringing them all back safely Mr MacDonald and at least I think Chloe is now well and truly over her crush!"

"Yes", I conceded, "that's one positive."

Rather amused he chuckled as he walked off towards his wife and daughter in the car. He half turned back to me still walking and chuckling.

"I told you Sir, slow and dead slow".

I could still smell a faint fetid stale smell in my hair for days afterwards.

BOI

I n the Heads of Year office, I had a folder called BOI, which basically stood for Bloody Ofsted Inspection. Ofsted inspections have changed dramatically since I first started teaching in the early 1990s. At that time, an Ofsted inspection would consist of a full week from Monday to Friday lunchtime, at which time the Lead Inspector would feedback to the school's Governing Body or at least the Chair of the Governing Body and the Headteacher. At the beginning of the week the core inspection team would be introduced to the apprehensive staff in the staff room by the equally apprehensive head teacher just so we knew who they were, we could identify faces and so on. The core team would be a Lead Inspector, in overall charge and a selection of other inspectors including lay inspectors. On top of that, would be various subject specialist inspectors for example a science inspector or humanities inspector and so on who would come in for part of the week to inspect and focus on that particular department with their specialist knowledge. So, it was a very stressful week for everyone. Ultimately, the Lead Inspector and one deputy would feedback a verbal grading with various added comments to the Chair of School Governors after lunch on the Friday then they would leave and go away and write up their report. It could, and still does, take up to two months for a report to be published on the Ofsted website and then becomes public knowledge. In the beginning there was seven grade options given by Ofsted for schools, just as there were seven grades for teaching lessons or should I say observing a teacher's lesson.

Ofsted inspections have changed dramatically over the years until the present time in 2023, an actual Ofsted inspection lasts less than two days.

Very much of the inspection determination seems to be done in advance by looking at DATA, DATA and MORE DATA. I am here talking specifically about England and not the other three countries in the United Kingdom. To be fair to the Department for Education, they have amassed lots and lots of data over the years and as information technology has become more sophisticated, they have data crunching specialists who can look at an infinite variety of outcomes for all sorts of students. Which is good and if one has the time, actually quite fascinating.

Is this better or worse than the original Ofsted style inspection of nearly a week on the ground IN the school, AT the chalkface? Yes, we did still use chalk in the early 1990s, before the proliferation of electronic whiteboards which have become cheaper, as most technology does over time.

Some teachers suspect that the move to shorter inspections is basically a money saving exercise. It is obviously cheaper. Ofsted inspectors have to be paid, have to be reimbursed their expenses, including overnight stays in hotels, travelling and so on.

In one sense the modern Ofsted inspection is essentially a type of franchise operation with a common framework. Companies submit a request to complete an Inspection.

Naturally most teachers, as much as they hate the stress of Ofsted inspections, would agree that there needs to be accountability, most of all to the tax payers who are paying for primary and secondary education. After all, teachers are taxpayers too and most of them will be parents, the older ones, grandparents and if they don't have children of their own, they will almost certainly have nieces and nephews. People forget that teachers have a vested interest in getting it right, not just because it's their career, but for those very personal reasons above.

The Ofsted framework has changed a lot overtime and regularly has a different focus, which means that schools are constantly in touch with each other to try and glean what has happened in a nearby school Ofsted inspection. Despite the fact, because of league tables, local schools are in competition with each other and by local we can mean over quite large catchment areas. Essex for example stretches from the Essex coast at the genteel Frinton-on-Sea and Clacton right down to the M25 orbital motorway, bordering London boroughs. It goes across a very rural agricultural part of Essex, up to Stansted Airport and back down again to the London area. So, it's quite possible for students to be sent by their parents from say the Chelmsford area to the Southend area to attend a state school or vice versa.

Essex also still has grammar schools which is another dynamic in the mix!

Many people, even teachers, seem to think that school inspections started with the formation of Ofsted under John Major's government. However, school inspections have been around since the mid-19th century with HM Inspectorate of Schools!

In 1837 two inspectors of elementary schools were appointed to monitor the effectiveness of an annual grant by Parliament set up in 1883 which provided what we now call primary school education for poor children.

Her Majesty's Inspectorate of Schools was set up in 1839. Her Majesty then being Victoria Regina. Eventually The Education Act of 1902 expanded inspections to secondary schools funded by the state.

Most school inspections however, prior to Ofsted's formation, were carried out by LEA inspectors employed by local councils.

Her/His Majesties Inspectorate, HMI mainly focused on writing general reports to the Secretary of State on Education across the country.

The same people usually think that performance related pay is a modern invention introduced under Michael Gove, however teachers were paid on results back in the 19th century which was usually accompanied by corporal punishment beatings and so on. That was the downside of performance related pay!

Introduced by Robert Lowe under Lord Palmerston's ministry in 1863, the system was called payment by results (PBR). However, this was abandoned after 30 years due to low morale of teachers and the increasing difficulty of recruiting teachers under this system. PBR has its dangers which people overlook.

One could say payment by results led to the Banking collapse of 2008!

In the USA, subprime mortgages were sold to individuals who had no hope or possibility of repaying them. Presumably the sales teams of these mortgage companies were getting bonuses for approving each mortgage application?

In any case school league tables in England have become more and more sophisticated and I have to admit if anyone has got the time to look at the league tables properly, they do give an awful lot of very good information.

Very detailed and pertinent information. However, the questions remain as to how many people, how many parents in particular, actually look at the league tables in detail or even the Ofsted inspection report in detail. They are just looking for the position in the league tables and also the Ofsted grading which is now a lot more crude in the sense that the gradings or ratings have changed from seven grades down to four.

Grade 1 = Outstanding.
Grade 2 = Good
Grade 3 = Requires Improvement (changed from Satisfactory)
Grade 4 = Inadequate (what used to be called Special Measures)

In the recent past however there have been schools which have not had a full (Section 5) inspection for 15 years. The state school that Ed Sheeran attended in the lovely town of Framlingham in Suffolk went from being Outstanding in an inspection in October 2006 to Inadequate in the November 2021 inspection.

So much for 'light touch' inspections for Outstanding schools, brought in during 2014 I believe.

Ed Balls did attempt to make School League Tables more nuanced by introducing a CVA column. Contextual Value Added. In other words the intake of a school was taken into account. Relative poverty, pupils on free school meals, housing density, special education needs as a percentage of the intake and much more. This gave more incentive to teachers and schools to 'add value' to their pupils and not just concentrate on raw results. CVA was abolished by the coalition government I think.

A marvellous moment sticks in my mind of an Ofsted inspection when I was a Head of Year in a boys' school. One of my Year group was waiting outside the Headteachers Office to complain about me for confiscating his mobile phone. I tried briefly to reason with him. Explaining that his phone would be safely placed in a sealed envelope in the school safe, he could have it at the end of the day. However, he was in a foul mood and in no humour to listen to me. On the other hand I had to get downstairs to give an assembly to my year group and fully expected an Ofsted inspector would be waiting at the back of the assembly hall with a clipboard to assess my assembly.

The Headteacher's office and the main school office were on the first floor at the top of a spiral staircase. I had to get downstairs fast and race around to the assembly. However, as I was going to turn down the stairs, I noticed another male Ofsted inspector coming out of the school office with his clipboard, having heard the pupil arguing with me at volume and demanding his phone back. As I was going down the staircase, I heard the boy shout at the top of his voice and directed at the said Ofsted inspector.

"What the f*** are you looking at mate?!"

I left them to it.

BOI II

O ver the years, in several schools, I have picked up various techniques for coping with Ofsted inspections. Just sob and beg for a good grade? No, be prepared, like a good Scout or Guide.

From using different shades of red ball point pen, for adding even more marking and feedback into pupils' books and folders. Not that I ever needed to do that obviously.

The use of a green pen has become the current fad over the last decade, for pupils to self-assess their own work from a mark scheme, in green pen. Such a fashion is often the result of one school getting an Ofsted report praising the self-assessment of work or the evaluation of work by students. This then gets taken up like wildfire in other schools around, whether it's appropriate or not.

I was told a long time ago, that letters written in green ink to the editor of a newspaper expressing wild or odd views were known as 'green ink letters', whether the ink was green or not! These days, I doubt many editors get any handwritten letters at all, in any coloured ink!

So green ink was in fashion now.

A rather ingenious trick by a teacher called Rebecca Barnard was explained to me thus.

She was an English teacher and a very good one indeed. She was also the Head of Year 11. In one of her Y11 classes, which was likely to get an inspection visit, she prewarned the class to put up their right hands if they knew the answer to a question and the left one if they didn't know. In any event, if she asked the class a question at the end of the lesson, ALL students were to put up their one hand. It meant that for the inspector at the rear of the class, he or she saw a remarkable level of 'engagement' in the class! A buzz word at the time. As well as a remarkable level of learning, apparently. All questions were answered perfectly. Luckily, the class liked Ms Barnard and she had a good relationship with them. That sort of adventure could easily go hideously wrong!

Ms Barnard was an interesting example of the development of a teacher. When she first came to the school as an NQT, (newly qualified teacher), she ended most days in tears at the way she was challenged and treated by classes. Often a friendly cleaner had to offer tea and sympathy after school. After a few years, perhaps she developed a thicker skin, but she became much less bothered by what the pupils said and would shout at them in the corridor without fear nor favour, if she felt they weren't following school rules. She became very quickly respected and liked by pupils and continued to be an excellent teacher.

Two Heads

It's not rare to find a Headteacher and other teachers on rota, outside the school gates at the end of the school day. This is certainly true of secondary schools.

Many people will remember the tragic death of Philip Lawrence, Headteacher of St Georges School in Maida Vale, London on the 8th of December 1995. Mr. Lawrence went to physically defend a 13-year-old black pupil, William Njoh, who was being attacked with an iron bar by a 15-year-old male pupil from another school.

In the process, Mr Lawrence was punched and then stabbed in the chest, he died later that evening in St Marys Hospital Paddington. Luckily such excessive brutality is very rare indeed. However even at the school I was employed at, in another part of London, there were risks.

Apart from the obvious risk of hundreds of children mixing with London traffic at the same time, we, as teachers keeping an eye on the pupils exiting the school, hopefully going home, would regularly see some shady characters hanging around. Not immediately outside the school gates, but maybe 100 or 200 yards away. They would approach students and offer them free drugs as a 'freebie', so called.

As far as we could see none of the students took these characters up on their skanky offer. They were of course offering very small quantities of drugs, free, to the students in the hope of getting them hooked and addicted to so-called soft or hard drugs. Thus, creating a ready future market for their dangerous and probably contaminated poisons.

Having recently read about the Prohibition era in the America of the

1920s, which was nothing less than a calamitous disaster, I am left wondering why we don't legalise some drugs. Not for children obviously, but at least a government could collect tax and ensure the purity of these often-exceedingly addictive substances and monitor them in a more effective way?

Not having studied that part of history much, I knew of Al Capone and the speakeasies, the St Valentine's Day Massacre and so on. I was shocked to find recently that Prohibition lasted such a very, very long time in the States. Beginning in 1920 and continuing until 1933! 13 years of utter bedlam and a boomtime for criminals, crooks and sleazebag corruption of all kinds. In New York, before Prohibition in 1920, there were about 14,500 saloons, yet by 1930, the Police Commissioner Whalen estimated there were at least 32,000 speakeasies within the same area, just ten years later!

In any case, back to a March day, after school, we were outside the school gates and that afternoon the days were definitely getting longer and visibly so now. We were joined by the Headteacher from a neighbouring secondary school who had just finished having a meeting with our Head, Mr Robins.

For whatever reason, a young tall black teenager from our school became indignant at having so many teachers around the school gates and after he was asked several times to leave the area and go home, he chose to aim a kick in the direction of the visiting Headteacher.

Obviously, this was in full view of hundreds of students in the vicinity. Although he didn't make contact, it was an insolent act on his part and potentially dangerous. William had come late into our school in Year 9 from Nigeria and in Year 10 we thought he was settling well at school. His father was a Pastor at a church not too many miles away.

Rather embarrassed by this incident, Mr Robins telephoned William's father and asked if he would come up for a meeting the next day after school, so that the incident could be discussed, and William could apologise to the neighbouring Headteacher.

A simple, quick and basic bit of restorative justice, an apology then everyone could move on.

The following afternoon, at about 4:00 PM, the two Headteachers convened and invited William's father into the Heads office with William himself, to discuss the previous days incident. They were expecting an apology and no more than a 5- or 10-minute meeting.

William's father listened in complete silence looking at his son who had his head bowed and looking at the two Headteachers sitting opposite. Once the explanation had finished, William's father looking at his son and speaking very softly and quietly but nevertheless clearly, said to his son.

"How dare you insult two great men like these gentlemen, who have got letters after their name, and who have risen into such an important position in the community. I am so embarrassed by this, that a son of mine would be so brash and impudent".

There was then a short pause of about 5 seconds and then much to the two Headteachers' surprise, William's father resumed.

"Boy, I want you to get down on your knees in front of these two honourable men and bow before them and beg forgiveness."

William stood up, he was quite a tall lad for Year 10, and he started to bend down to go onto his knees when Mr Robins, shocked, astonished and mortified at this sudden turn of events interposed.

Gently pulling William back up straight and gesturing for him to sit back down in his chair, he hesitantly spoke.

"Really that won't be required and it's not appropriate, we just wanted an apology and for you, William to agree that this type of behaviour will not happen again."

So, William apologised to the two Heads in turn and then looked at his father for further clarification as to what he should do next. Just as before, his father quietly spoken, told him to stand up, as he himself stood up and they thanked Mr Robins and his colleague and quietly left the office.

Mr Robins and the neighbouring Head were left flabbergasted and stunned and it became clearer as to why William was finding it harder to appreciate discipline and respect for adults in his new country.

Charlie Newman

I had a student called Charlie Newman in my Year group whose brother had recently made the big time in English cricket. His brother, Jim, was being paid loads of money by his club and was about to go on tour with England. Charlie was at the same time immensely proud but also perceptibly jealous of his older brother. He resented his brother Jim for achieving his dream as Charlie wasn't quite at that level. Presumably the parents had decided to keep Charlie at his state comprehensive, as he was already there before his brother made it big. Charlie also had friends and was doing reasonably well academically and very well in sports teams.

In order to compensate his kid brother for his clear and maybe understandable jealousy of him, Jim would give Charlie, on occasions, lots of gifts and so on.

We had to deal with a tricky situation when unknown to the teaching staff, 14-year-old Charlie came in one day with £300 in cash, which his brother had given him to purchase a new, much pursued, pair of brand new trainers after school in town.

Bearing in mind this was the early 2000s, it was even more money at that time than it is now. However apparently Charlie couldn't resist playing the big shot and was waving around his wads of cash in the air in front of his mates, fifteen £20 notes splayed out and showing them all.

"Hey look what I got from Jim, I'm gonna get some sick trainers after school, sorted".

Unfortunately, none of the teaching staff or the admin staff had any idea about this until we got a call from Charlie's dad, understandably furious that his son's money, £300 in cash, had gone missing from the PE changing rooms during the day. I didn't find out until the end of the day, as I had a full day teaching. Which made it very difficult for me, as Head of Year to investigate, as at that time many of the pupils had gone home.

Dad demanded a meeting with me and the Headteacher immediately he got off work and he wanted answers. I did my best in the minutes I had, talking to some other pupils in his year group. Boys obviously, as they had a separate changing room, to find out if anyone had heard any rumours of the missing cash. Very often children will talk and it's not too difficult to track down a culprit if a theft occurs.

I was getting nothing however from ringing the boys at home. I also risked the wrath of other parents, making it sound as if I was accusing their son of stealing!

In any case Charlie's dad arrived bang on 5:30 PM and by then the school was virtually deserted. I waited downstairs to meet the dad whose name was Dave. He was still fuming that this extent of money had gone missing and not been found. He was banging the table in the Headteacher's study and demanding answers or full compensation.

When he had calmed down a bit, I explained what had happened with Charlie flashing his cash after he came to school in the morning, but the fact that school staff were only aware of this when it was too late.

The dad was extremely straight talking so I took a risk and decided to play bad cop to the Headteacher's good cop. I knew that the Headteacher could turn on the charm and could probably smooth it over.

"It was a bloody stupid thing to give Charlie £300 cash to bring into school don't you think? Why on earth didn't someone tell the school he had that amount of cash? I've got three children myself, I would never give them that amount of money in cash to come into school, well not without fore-warning the school. Seriously!"

I expressed my amazement and annoyance, which were real. I was fairly annoyed, I was supposed to be attending a play at my daughters school at 6pm.

Dad seemed a bit non plussed by this attack. I explained in all truthfulness, it would be very unlikely now that we would be able to find the cash, as the pupils had all gone home. It would be pointless searching them tomorrow morning! That is very time consuming and fraught with latent hostility. Maybe not so latent.

Dad then tried another tack,

"How do we know it was one of these pupils, it could have been one of the teachers?" The Headteacher explained that if that was true, it would be clear grounds for dismissal and a serious stain on a teachers CV. It would have to be disclosed in references and for that reason it would be very unlikely for a teacher to risk their career for £300, apart from the fact he didn't believe his PE teachers were dishonest!

£300 is a massive amount of cash for a 14-year-old boy, but not really a lot to a teacher if it ended his or her career, not to even mention calling into question the ethics and professionalism of the teacher.

I took another risk and got up out of my chair and opened the door to the main school office, which was adjacent to the Headteachers Study. We could all see a medium sized bright blue cast iron safe on the floor, in between several blue filing cabinets.

"If you had told us Mr Newman, that Charlie was coming into school with £300 in cash we could have put it in the school safe securely and returned it to him at the end of the school day, so he could go and buy his trainers, although I wouldn't be too happy having a 14 year old wandering around town with that much cash in his pocket, if he was my son!"

Charlie's dad sat back in his seat and breathed out a sigh of frustration and grudging acceptance.

"Yeah, I suppose you're right, I'm sorry we should have told the school. His brother was just trying to make Charlie feel good. He's a bit jealous of his older brother.

"Yes, we had noticed" added the Head wryly.

"Jim's obviously not short of money. It's coming out of his ears. Okay, okay, we'll leave it at that" Mr Newman resolved.

The Headteacher promised that we would continue to keep our ears to the ground in the hope we might get a lead on who had taken the money, but he insisted in all frankness, we could not be very hopeful now.

"Would you like us to get the police involved Mr Newman?"

"No, no, no, no, no, we're not short of money, far from it. It's not worth wasting police time, we'll just have to put it down to experience."

We all shook hands, and we left it at that. I escorted him back out to his car, a top of the range Jaguar. Was that another gift from Jim?

I realise that Mr Newman was a decent chap, I can't really remember what he did for a living, but he was clearly struggling with the newfound super wealth of his eldest son and trying to manage the ensuing friction between him and his younger son.

Mr Newman always came to stand pitch-side when Charlie was playing for the school soccer team at home matches. I was told a few weeks later that when he heard one of the fathers of an opposition team player making racist noises towards one the black youngsters on our school team, he went up to him and despite being considerably shorter than the other parent, he told him in no uncertain terms that he would deck him if he ever heard any more language or noises like that. As I say he was a decent man and straight talking.

Odours and Cold

G etting the pupils onto the free buses provided by Gourock Council was not easy. Very few pupils were used to queuing in anything remotely like a line. The deputy head had some fraught days after school getting the buses loaded! He had to think of a simple and cheap system. He came up with a raffle ticket type of approach.

A different colour each day at random and the pupils had to sit down in the canteen if they wanted to be given a ticket. It basically worked and turned an unruly mob into a faintly manageable mob for the 10 or 15 mins it took to load up the buses for the 2-mile trip down to Mirebury.

In the freezing winter days, with the sun dropping over the horizon in the west, the wind blew in an icy fresh blast of air, each time we opened the glass door and let out 20 or so pupils with their raffle tickets so they could board the bus.

On one occasion a loud and extremely gobby Year 10 girl screamed out "shut the f*****g door, its freezing" as another group were sent out with their tickets to the double decker bus outside.

Immediately a boy in the same year group shouted out in an equally loud voice from the next table.

"Shut your f*****g legs it smells of fish" towards the girl. She became much quieter and the embarrassed teaching staff pretended they didn't hear, to save her blushes. The boy was spoken to quietly about the inappropriateness of his comment in a discrete way. We had to suppress our laughter and shock at the outrageousness of his sheer rudeness. They were probably related.

Inappropriate is certainly an overused word in schools. What it really means is:

"Your behaviour or language is utterly unacceptable in a civilised society; how dare you act and speak like that".

Unfortunately, such direct chastisement will usually result in a complaint from the same's parents and in the moment, the situation would probably escalate, because some of the pupils were wound up like coiled springs most of the time. Ready to explode.

As difficult as they were, I did wonder what sort of home life they endured.

In The Bin

O ne of the duties of an assistant headteacher would be to act as the person responsible for one of the sites on a split site school. Depending on the timetable of other senior teachers and the whereabouts of the Headteacher, you could be the only senior teacher on that site for a morning or even a whole day. Effectively acting Headteacher. A sure and easy laxative.

Usually accompanied by a radio which had contact with the site reception and with the other site 3 miles away, you had to roam the corridors and be a presence around the school (or technically half a school). Sadly, many issues involved pupils just running out of class or asking to go to the toilet and not returning.

Fundamentally a small number of pupils preferred running around the school trying to disrupt other classes and generally causing mayhem. In any case this was a danger for them, as they were out of the supervision of a teacher or even an adult.

So we had to effectively find them and get them back into class or into isolation.

The isolation room is a system many schools use to sanction pupils who are repeatedly disrupting other pupils learning. Schools have different names for a similar procedure. Isolation room. Reflection room. Consequence room. Removal room. Different names for a similar system.

They sit in cubicles facing the wall so unable to distract or be distracted and have their classwork taken to them each lesson. The room itself had its own toilet facilities and was heated in the winter and with aircon in the summer.

Really it was a useful resource for any school. Pupils had to have their lunches in the room so isolated from their mates, which was probably the main punishment. The isolation room was always staffed by two qualified teachers and an LSA. It allowed pupils to focus on their work and allowed the class teacher back in the home classroom to concentrate their teaching on the other 29 or so pupils who wanted to get on, learn and make progress.

I saw this type of system in many schools., not least when I retired and worked as a supply teacher. The most effective schools I saw always ran their system rigorously and with a crystal clear structure. Basically, three strikes and you're out.

A warning was given in class to a pupil, then a second if they didn't conform to the classroom expectations and on a third warning the teacher would request the on-call teacher, either by sending an email to reception or better still some schools have a button on the teachers laptop screen that can be pressed. It should be seamless.

In the best schools it is seamless and very effective. It relies on the classroom teacher implementing the system well and not jumping up the warning system too quickly and in many cases, it doesn't need to be used at all in a class lesson. Students who are removed are set a detention after school the same day. Parents informed. Hallelujah for parents mobile phones. Senior teachers collecting students towards the end of the last lesson so they cannot run off.

However, it always has to be set alongside a proper functioning Rewards system.

A Rewards ladder.

Anyone who thinks that teenagers will not respond to getting merits or reward points is wrong, wrong, wrong. They do almost 99% of the time. They may not like receiving them in front of their peers, but they do appreciate them.

Schools which fail badly only have a sanctions ladder without a well-developed rewards ladder. It is frustrating to see as a supply teacher how easily behaviour could be improved.

The adage that rewards should outstrip sanctions by a ratio of 7 to 1 is probably an exaggeration. This is often a figure promoted by educationalists, but certainly there should be a greater emphasis on rewards.

Why do supermarkets and petrol companies and other consumer brands use Rewards? Because even adults respond. Tesco Clubcard points. Nectar points, BP, Shell reward points and so on. People like to be recognised and appreciated.

We received a new tea towel through the post from Sainsburys recently. Packaged nicely. It must have cost pennies, but it's a nice gesture. Human beings like to be acknowledged and valued. If only for shopping! How many adults feel utterly delighted at being praised by their boss or line manager in front of colleagues?

Some may pretend they don't care but they do!

Likewise with teenagers they may feign indifference or even cynicism, but they do like being rewarded. They ABSOLUTELY DO! I promise you.

Some schools have well developed rewards systems and get local companies to sponsor tokens from Amazon or iTunes or well, it doesn't really matter. It works.

It has to be managed properly and you will hear the saying.

"We mustn't devalue the points" by giving them out too freely. Which is true. However, in some cases it's a code for a minority of lazy teachers not to get with the programme.

Anyway, back to walking the corridors with a radio, trying not to make it look too much like a prison. A very tiny minority of these children really do have no 'reasonable' switch.

If they feel like leaving a lesson, they will. Much as a school would like to just leave them doing whatever they need to do, roaming the corridors, they are children, some of them 6ft 2 in Year 11, nevertheless children.

We need to know where they are and get them back into the relevant classroom or inclusion room. As well as stopping them disrupting the learning of the vast majority of students who want to learn. I was doing one of these, in loco parentis, senior manager sweeps of the site and I could not find a Year 9 girl Kayley. How many spellings of Kayley have I seen over the years. Kayley, Kaleigh, Caleigh, Calie, Calee. Yes really, all pronounced in the same manner. She had asked to go to the toilet from a Maths lesson and not returned.

In any case I couldn't find this Kayley anywhere. I went to the reception and had a look at the various CCTV cameras around the site. Cameras there to protect the children, (and staff) from intruders. I could not see her anywhere. Had she climbed over one of the gates. (Again, locked to prevent intruders).

I returned to my search, all the while picking up calls across both sites on the radio. I happened to pass another teacher, Neil, on a free period on the way to the toilet.

I asked him if he had seen Kayley. "Nope," he sounded in a hurry. Those flapjacks at breaktime from the school canteen may have been a bit too high in fibre.

"Try the bins by the kitchen".

"What?" I replied confused and with growing alarm.

"The big bins, large kitchen waste bins for the food waste".

I watched as he continued down the corridor, expecting him to turn his head with a smile and say, "just joking."

He didn't. I walked briskly to the school kitchen area and found two large cylindrical metal bins on wheels, over 6 ft high and 3 ft diameter. I shouted "Kayley, you in there"? This was surreal.

No reply. I went to the other bin and tried the same searching question. I really felt like a plank as cars were passing on the road outside the fence and some drivers must be wondering why a grown man in a suit was talking to a large commercial kitchen bin!

This was ridiculous. Surely, in order to avoid going to a lesson, Kayley had not climbed into a stinking bin of boiled cabbage, custard, gravy and whatever is thrown out from school kitchens.

Surely not. The bin was too high for me to see into it even with my 6ft 2in of height and tiptoes. I tried, nevertheless. Those cars kept driving by.

I radioed the caretaker to bring a stepladder to the kitchen area.

"Oh, Kayley B gone missing again?" he volunteered. I didn't want the other senior staff listening on the other site. I'd mislaid a student! In a bin?

"Just bring a stepladder Joe please, asap, I know your busy".

Joe and stepladder arrived, and I climbed up to look down into the bin. Just gunk and foul-smelling days old food. I think the bins were collected twice a week.

We moved the ladder to the second bin, up I went and looked down.

"Hello Sir," Kayley smiled up at me. "You took your bleeding time. Good game though, whatdya think?"

I was pretty much lost for words. Kayley climbed out of the bin somehow and onto the ladder. She seemed elated that she had gone unnoticed for so long. As if she had put one over on the school.

I told her rather flatly that the bin was full of germs and the only person she had cheated was herself, ...out of a lesson!

Mum was called up to collect her for home and try to clean her up.

"Well, I can't clean her uniform that quick, can I."

I replied that it would be fine if Kayley returned in a tracksuit. Just for today.

Mum turned to Kayley when she arrived.

"What you do that for, you silly mare, I hope you wasn't eating out of the bin?"

My stomach muscles hardened.

She does this every few weeks Mr MacDonald, I think it's when her periods are bad.

I kept quiet. Off they went home to return Kayley, hopefully in an hour, smelling rather sweeter. There's only so much Febreze can do, let's face it!

Never encountered that before or since. Nonetheless, Kayley was referred on to social services and CAMHS.

Inappropriate

T his word inappropriate is probably one of the most frequently used words in modern British schools.

As in a teacher saying to a parent at parents evening,

"Your son/daughter, (delete as appropriate) has had a large number of sanctions this term for using inappropriate language in class"

In reality, a teacher is saying, "your son/daughter is disturbingly foul-mouthed and has been warned on numerous occasions about using obscenities in front of other pupils or teachers, its offensive and distracting to other pupils. What the heck is happening at home?"

It would be unwise to take the second line, as many parents do not take kindly to having their parenting skills being called into question. Especially as other parents could possibly overhear the conversation at a parents evening. It is unlikely the Headteacher of the school would back up a teacher if such a parent made a complaint. Therein lies the problem. Straight talking would be more useful, for everyone.

An incident that comes to mind and turned out to be hilariously funny in context, was a lesson I had with a group of Year 10 students. As they were entering the classroom at the start of the lesson, I was moving around, handing out exercise books, when two Year 10 boys entered, clearly in the middle of a conversation they had started in the corridor on the way to my lesson. Goodness know how it began! All I heard as they entered the room was Jamie telling David.

"Yeah, I wouldn't mind taking ********* up the anus!" Fill in the blanks with a famous female pop star of the time. I genuinely can't remember who.

Disturbed from handing out books and generally welcoming students to my science lab.

I interjected "Woah, woah, woah, that's totally inappropriate. That conversation ends now."

As other boys and girls came into my lab, Jamie threw his hands up into the air proclaiming.

"Sir, what's wrong now! You're always moaning at me. I can't do anything right. We haven't even sat down yet and you're having a go at us, I used the proper word, anus, that's a scientific word. You taught us that in Year 8!"

I confirmed that it was indeed a proper scientific and medical term, but that I wasn't bothered about the term anus, but rather his imagery and actions around said anus. The other students arriving in the lab must have been wondering what on earth we were talking about and more importantly why!

Jamie who was particularly tall for Year 10, with a shock of unruly blond hair, sat down grumpily in his place at the front of the class where I placed him to keep an eye on him. He totally failed to understand the inappropriateness of his comments.

"Above the anus is the rectum, then the colon, Jamie offered. "See, I did learn it!"

I tried to distract him as the rest of the class continued to pile in.

"Excellent Jamie, that's good. So, what comes above the colon?" I wasn't sure why we were going backwards up the digestive tract but anyway anything to get away from his focus on anal intercourse.

"Er, I don't know Sir"

It begins with I, Jamie.

"You Sir?"

No, the letter I, Jamie"

"Is it intestines Sir?"

"Well, it's all intestines, Jamie!"

OK, at least I had successfully changed the subject and we could start the lesson.

I wondered why Jamie was so up on the lower part of the gut. Perhaps his dad was an Gastroenterologist? No, his father was an electrician I remembered. A good one so I heard.

I tried again to explain to him at the end of the lesson why his initial conversation was inappropriate but had to give up as I was close to laughing out loud.

Robocop

As part of the Safer Schools Initiative, the County Council and Midshire Police worked together with an onsite police officer, PC Rachel Stock.

So the County Council paid half her salary and Midshire Police paid the other half. It worked well for both parties. PC Stock was in full uniform and stood with the senior teachers at the school gates welcoming students to school in the morning and saw them off home at the gates after school. She gained the soubriquet RoboCop not unexpectedly. However, she was not a PCSO but a fully trained Police Officer with all the powers one would expect of a Police Officer in uniform.

It is truly amazing how much information can be gleaned from school pupils who seemed to think that no one is listening, as they have their loud conversations in corridors or playground. The area around the school was highlighted as a high crime hotspot. PC Rachel Stock was always smiling but always had an ear to the ground. She worked 9.00 till 3:30 five days a week and presumably had a regular debrief back at Pilstown police station. She garnered a lot of useful information beneficial in preventing crime.

On the whole, the pupils liked the police officer to be on site and were more reassured by her presence than the opposite. As happens occasionally when a pupil needs to be removed from a lesson to the isolation room, they may refuse to leave. Admittedly this was very rare indeed. However, I can remember two occasions that PC Stock had to go down to a classroom and remove a student from the class.

In schools which didn't have the luxury of an on-site police officer, for the very rare occasions when a pupil refused to leave the classroom or lab, we had to remove the other 29 students to an empty classroom, if we could find one nearby and continue the lesson in that way. An LSA or teacher sitting with the now isolated student.

Again, this was very rare indeed, in fact I can only remember two circumstances in my career that this had to be done.

If a student has used particularly foul language towards a teacher, then there needs to be a consequence.

Ignoring it will only make it happen again.

I recall an incident when a female Year 11 student had been particularly obnoxious and disruptive. After several warnings I asked her to wait outside the classroom whilst I found the on-call teacher.

Her parting shot to me as she was walking out of the room was shouting at the top of her voice and directed at me.

"You can f**k me up the arse" much to the jubilation of the rest of the class.

Not really a very sensible parting shot to a class of hormonal teens!

It's times like that, when you long to be unprofessional.

It would have been so easy to make an equally inappropriate comment which would have slapped her down metaphorically. So many options for a response!

I resisted and literally bit my tongue so hard I almost drew blood.

Sit In or Sit On

As many teachers will know there is a continual problem with 'school-refusers'.

Pupils who will not attend school for whatever reason. The longer they have off school the more difficult it will be to reintegrate them. It's a vicious circle.

I know myself I detested secondary school in the first year as an eleven-year-old or Year 7, as its been called now for decades. However, by Year 8 I loved school, had made friends, and felt really at home.

Inevitably the local education authority truant officer or Educational Welfare Officer will get involved when attendance is poor. Figures are reported in league tables.

First the school will call home and try to find out about the issues. Several calls later they will have a reintegration plan to get pupil X back into the school. If the pupil still does not turn up the EWO will get involved and start communicating with home, then arrange a home visit.

Some EWOs will only visit with another person as a witness. Occasionally what has been said is remembered in diverse ways by the various parties. Recollections may vary. As the late Queen put it so wisely.

Even if the parents are cooperating, it is difficult to get a result. Anything under 95% attendance is a problem.

So next steps will be legal action, in England anyway. I'm sure Wales, Northern Ireland and Scotland have very similar systems.

Parents will be issued with fines which can escalate. Often this is enough to improve attendance. For many years attendance has been reported in league tables and quite rightly. Taxpayers are paying for state education, and they have a right to know if pupils are turning up! The quality of education they get is a whole other matter.

We had an issue when a parent was genuinely doing their best to get their son into school. A quite large Year 10 boy called Terry. I refer to his size for a reason.

He turned up one day with dad. Dad had somehow persuaded Terry to get up, get dressed, put on his uniform and go to school with him. The dad was at his wits end and petrified by more legal action. At this particular school I was an Assistant Headteacher and happened to be in the foyer of the school when they turned up at 8.30am. Delighted to see him, I welcomed Terry back and was just about to talk to an equally delighted dad about how we would reintegrate Terry, when Terry seeing an opportunity as his dad relaxed for a split second, turned on his heels and ran back out of the foyer heading for the school gates. Dad pursued him gainfully. We had a piece of manicured lawn, well grassed, outside in front of the foyer. Dad grabbed his son Terry and pulled him to the ground. Luckily it was bone dry as it hadn't rained for a while. Dad proceeded to sit on top of Terry, shouting.

"I aint getting no more fines for you, my son".

As I said Terry was large and it was the only way his dad could restrain him. As the bell went, I had to rush across the school to give an assembly. I handed over to the Deputy Headteacher, who luckily was the School Designated Safeguarding Lead for the school. Whatever happened, Terry did not appear in classes, and it appears went home after all. This was one frustrated parent trying to do the correct thing.

Clearly, we couldn't physically restrain the boy to keep him in school.

Really difficult issues to deal with. Often poor attendance is with the collusion of parents. They want their offspring to stay at home for a delivery. Or to look after pre-schoolers. Often, I knew that parents were keeping their children at home for company because they themselves felt lonely and anxious. Easy to condemn and it really isn't a solution, but sometimes it's hard as a parent I imagine to hold the self-discipline to get your child into school if you are feeling weak and needy yourself.

Unacceptable, but what are the solutions? People tend to blame 'the cuts' even when there haven't been any cuts or 'the government', of whichever party or parties is in power.

We had one girl who was a school refuser which went on for weeks and weeks if not months. Eventually the EWO went to the home. Gained access. Which means she was allowed in. Mum showed her around the small two bedroomed flat. No beds at all present. A sofa. No beds. This was reported back to me as Head of Year. I was astonished in my naivety and inexperience. I phoned social services the same day. After a bit of arguing, I got the Council to buy a bed and mattress for the girl at least, who was 14 years old. I was self-satisfied that weekend. I had fought the good fight and result! However, the girl still did not show up at school the following week. The EWO visited again the following week and finds the bed and mattress sold. Mum said, "I needed fags didn't I, what'd you expect me to do?"

When I found out I rang the social services again, rather more humbly this time and sheepishly relayed what had happened. The social worker was clearly not surprised in the slightest.

"What exactly did you expect us to do, put a tracker on the divan and mattress?".

I mumbled apologies, although it wasn't my fault. That's £200 the social services don't have in their budget anymore.

Fingering

Working in my classroom one early morning before school, I heard a commotion somewhere outside my classroom in the corridor. This was probably about 7:45 am and I had been at my desk since about 7:15 am. There is, by the way, a strange myth that teachers only work between nine and three, five days a week. It amazes me that this myth persists, as most people only have to look at school car parks early in the morning to see them filling up from about 7:30 am. At the latest. Primary or Secondary.

I worked with a teacher who was at his desk at 6:00 am every single morning. He lived about 8 miles from school. He did all his lesson preparation, marking and reports, so he could leave more or less 10 minutes after the students left at the end of the school day, unless he had a meeting. He obviously didn't need to take any work home either on weekday evenings or weekends. He was a real morning person!

Anyway, back to the commotion. I reluctantly dragged myself away from what I was doing i.e., marking and fine-tuning lessons. Went out into the corridor to find a very distressed Year 9 pupil called Bianca. I've changed the name obviously. There were probably about a dozen students in the corridor who would normally just chat or whatever they wanted to do before school. Often charging up their phones in the corridor plug sockets meant for the cleaning staff vacuum cleaners. This, they were not allowed to do. I even found one morning a group of 14-year-old girls sitting on the corridor floor near my classroom with electric hair-curlers plugged into the wall!

I confiscated them, if only for their own safety and rang home to explain they shouldn't be brought to school. They belonged to Jessica.

"We was running late Mr MacDonald, I'm sorry, she won't fetch them in again."

Fair enough.

Pretty annoyed to find that the same girl, Jessica did not have a pen, pencil, ruler or any equipment for my lesson later in the day! She did have electric hair curlers though! Or rather now she didn't, as they were in the school safe awaiting collection. So, a very truculent Jessica kept giving me 'evils' as the kids say, throughout the lesson.

The school canteen was open from 6:30 am anyway, serving breakfasts for students and staff.

Sorry, I got distracted dear reader.

I found Bianca outside in the corridor in a frenzy shouting at the top of her voice very loudly.

"He didn't finger me, he didn't finger me, I promise"

Which is a bit of a shock to the senses at quarter to eight in the morning. A number of boys were milling around, and a couple were doubled up laughing at her reaction which of course she was making even worse, by telling even more people inadvertently. Apparently to tease her, one devious boy pupil had messaged out that Bianca's 'boyfriend' had been allowed to finger her the previous evening on the way home from school.

Probably completely fabricated obviously, but Bianca's reaction, shouting what she said at the top of her voice really wasn't helping matters.

I managed to calm her down and she explained the above to me with no hint of embarrassment. I suggested I take her to a female member of staff who she could talk to and that it was best not to talk about it in front of other pupils at all!

Fortunately, I found a woman teacher three classrooms along and explained the situation to Mrs Brigstock. Although Bianca wasn't in the slightest bit embarrassed, I admit I did feel a bit uncomfortable, but the matter needed to be knocked on the head quickly before it got out of control.

I left Bianca with Mrs Brigstock and proceeded back to my classroom where all the other pupils had hightailed it, expecting to get the blame. Later in the day after a bit of detective work which wasn't that difficult, the Year 9 pastoral staff identified the boy and he was sent home. A conversation was had with his mother on the phone, thankfully not by me and Mum was understandably mortified. This is what is known as a fixed term exclusion, in this case, for one day. As far as I'm aware that was the end of the matter and I didn't hear more about it which I would have done as I taught Bianca and I vaguely knew her mother.

Well, if you must come in early to work you expect to have to pick up these other extraneous matters! I could have stayed in my room, continued to work and ignored the commotion, which I must admit I very nearly did. However, you learn as a teacher that you are acting *in loco parentis* even BEFORE the school day has officially started!

Now this is an interesting concept.

One of the few bits of Latin I got on my year-long teacher training course! It translates as "in the place of a parent".

Originally from English Common law, it was part of the Elementary Education Act 1870.

From the Children Act 1989

Teachers must behave as any reasonable parent would do in promoting the welfare and safety of children in their care.

So proper. Yet an awful lot rides on that label reasonable!

Vince and the Vaccines

"I do not, under any circumstances want Vince to have a vaccine Mr MacDonald"

Mrs Windlass was referring to her son Vincent standing plumply next to her.

The school vaccination service was coming into school to vaccinate a whole group of pupils. Clearly forms must be sent out to parents and parents had to approve the vaccines and sign to give their consent.

This was back in the mid-1990s. As far as I can remember these vaccines were for adolescent tetanus and diphtheria. I may be wrong. It was a jab anyway or a jag as they say in Scotland. However, this was all the remit of the school vaccination service and effectively the school was just being used as a convenient venue to secure a large number of pupils in one morning or afternoon session. Qualified nurses were sent into the school, so that hundreds of pupils were vaccinated quickly and effectively. Then they move on to the next school. Cost effective and uncontentious hopefully. You would think.

However, Mrs Windlass who was quite a forceful parent, in all the wrong modes, was clear for whatever reason, she didn't want Vince to have any vaccinations. Vince didn't seem to have a lot of say in it, but that was her prerogative as a parent. The brief conversation with Mrs Windlass took place in the foyer of the school as she recognised me as Vince's form tutor from Parents Evening and fair enough, she made it very clear she did not give permission for the vaccination. She didn't have to give me a reason. Vince was with her. I told him that it was crystal clear that he wasn't to have the vaccine. He nodded agreement.

Generally, vaccines are given in subject classes to the pupils, so they are not pulled from a variety of classes. Which would cause maximum disruption. My form session was first thing in the morning after registration at 8:50. I had all the signed forms from the parents which came back in to school and my class was sent for, as a prefect came to collect them, to go to the school gymnasium where the nurses were set up. There were about three students whose parents hadn't returned the form, so they would have to be vaccinated by their gp's surgery if they wanted it at all. I lined up my 12-year-olds, handed out their forms and told Vince and the two others to wait in the classroom.

I would be back as soon as I had delivered my form class to the nurses. However, Vince insisted on coming with us. He appeared to be quite a spoiled boy, and was used to getting his own way. He kept nagging me and nagging me.

"Please Sir, I just want to go with my friends, I know my mum doesn't want me to have the vaccination, but I just want to go with them, that's all then I'll come back." Time was ticking, so I agreed Vince could go with us and wait with his friends only but must not have the vaccination! He didn't have a signed form anyway. I marched the 28 pupils across the quadrangle to the door of the school gym. As soon as I had delivered 28 students to the gym which was set up with four nurse stations, I rushed back to my form room to be with the two students I'd briefly left there. The first students were already getting their immunisation and would be heading back in a few seconds. I made a point of indicating Vince to the nurse on the door and that his mother did not give permission and he was just accompanying his friends, that's all. He was not to have the vaccination.

Back in the form room I didn't have to wait long for the inoculated pupils to start dribbling back in twos and threes, excitedly rubbing their arms gently and each other's arms not so gently, chatting about the fleeting experience. Once settled, they carried on with their day.

The next morning all hell broke loose, as I was summoned to the Headteachers Office and barked at for 15 minutes. Vince had been given the vaccine despite my best efforts and no signed form, and his mother was picking bits of carpet out of her teeth.

She was threatening to sue the school, the LEA, me, the NHS and anyone else she could think of at the time.

What a depressing incident. Obviously, Vince had been herded into the gym and given the vaccine by some harassed nurses trying their best to get through as many 12-year-olds as possible. He knew full well he wasn't to have it. Nevertheless, he was only 12. If I had stayed until all my class were pinged in the arm, there was a risk that the ones left in the classroom or the pupils returning to the classroom could have been injured if left unattended. That would have been my fault. Sometimes Senior Management in schools don't think things through. As I was years later to become one of them, I now know the pressures.

In any case I heard no more about it. Not a peep. I don't know if Mrs Windlass had objected on medical grounds or other grounds, but Vince was in school every day and apart from me being 'persona non grata' for a week or two, no one suffered any ill effects.

The last I heard on the grapevine was that an adult Vince was running a strip club in East London.

Make-Up and
Snow Show

After I retired one of the agencies I was working with, asked me if I would do a longer placement at a school on the coast. This was intended to be only three days a week, but a fixed term contract until the end of the academic year. January to July.

It was at this school I had my first encounter with a transgender boy who wore full make up to school every day, Troy was in Year 8, quite a small boy for January of Year 8. Mascara, eyeliner, blusher on his cheeks, lipstick. The whole collection. This was about the mid-2010s and the debate on trans issues had not really detonated. Thankfully.

Troy was undeniably quite a short boy but had a very large personality and the other boys really didn't know what to make of him, as well as the fact that he was larger than life, he also had a very sharp tongue. Whether that was his natural personality or a defence mechanism, it certainly worked well, in that most of the boys stayed clear of him and many of the girls were quite protective.

I didn't have the pleasure of teaching him, as he wasn't on my timetable and I didn't really know a lot about him or his history and as I was going to be at the school for only 6 months at the most, there was consequently not a lot of time to get to know him. This was, coincidentally, a school in Ofsted Grade 4, therefore in Special Measures and with very challenging behaviour indeed.

The behaviour was so difficult that I went to the Headteacher about every two weeks and said I was resigning at the end of the week. As I was working through an agency there was no long notice period. She managed to persuade me to continue. In the end, I survived to the end of the summer term somewhat shattered and bruised. At the end of the academic year over 20 teaching staff left, including the Headteacher, Mrs Jones who took a demotion to become Deputy Head in another school. It was a complicated environment.

As is often the case in a challenging school, there was a lot of running around corridors during lessons. Internal truancy if you like. Troy was often one of the culprits and very easy to spot as he had more make up on than any of the older girls!

By February it was 'proper winter' as the pupils would say. It started snowing about 10.15am. Inevitably the questions start.

"Are we going to be sent home Sir?"

"Is Mrs Jones going to close the school Sir?"

"Will we get snowed in, Miss?"

Pupils rushing to the windows to look at the snow, which then took a good 5 minutes to get them back in their seats and on task.

A message was sent round by email by 10.30am from Mrs Jones

"I am not closing the school and we are not finishing early, please inform students."

By midday the snow was not easing off and was in fact getting deeper and heavier. It was settling on the ground.

It was looking ugly. Well it looked quite beautiful. It's amazing how much noise the snow absorbs. Everything seems quieter. We were at risk of getting utterly snowed in. Spending the night supervising 1000 teens and pre-teens was not a prospect any of the staff appreciated thinking about, let alone doing.

Sure, enough Mrs Jones, a woman not stubborn enough to stick to her original decision, in the face of changing facts, relented, after having telephoned the local authority and looked at the weather forecast for the rest of the day. The problem with a seaside town is that there is usually only one, sometimes two roads in and out! The admin staff were sent around to inform the students to leave and go straight home. Details to parents would be sent out by text.

Once we got the students off site, the teachers raced for their cars in the hope of getting a space on the road out of town. It took me 3 hours to get home.

Falsies

Statistically, which subject in schools do you think has the most accidents or injuries? You would be wise to possibly think it was Science, however the statistics show that it is in fact, physical education or PE. Which does makes sense.

Despite the sometimes-extraordinary risks taken in Science lessons in secondary schools, there is also, alongside the risk, a lot of risk assessment going on in the background. In fact, notwithstanding all the glassware, the use of potentially dangerous chemicals, electricity, and even microbes used, there are thankfully very few accidents in British secondary school science labs, and I would imagine it's the same elsewhere in other countries. When you have upwards of 30 pupils, sometimes more, milling around a Science lab, conducting experiments can certainly be a useful purgative for a teacher.

In fact, by far the most common accident is probably pupils swinging on their lab stools backwards and falling off. Always good for a laugh for the rest of the class and thankfully I never saw anyone crack their head open on the bench behind. I have heard of it happening and a cracked scalp or skull produces a shocking amount of blood! I witnessed a few near misses certainly.

Many pupils still equate ANY liquid chemical used in a Science lesson, with the feared 'acids'. In fact, in my first week as Head of Science in a challenging school, I had prepared, or rather the science technicians had prepared, a simple experiment, with dilute hydrochloric acid. When I explained what we were going to do, comparing the reactions of various metals with hydrochloric acid, there was a stunned silence amongst the Year 9 pupils and a few whispers. Remember this was my very first week in this school.

I let the silence rest for a few seconds, then raised my eyebrows asking for an explanation of this unusual bashfulness.

One Year 9 boy put his hand up and disclosed,

"Oh, we were banned for using acids before, as we used to throw it in each other's faces!"

"I see," trying to hide my shock. "Well, that won't be happening today!" I exclaimed.

Well hopefully not. I could feel my calves tighten with tension.

As I say a useful bowel loosener.

In truth, the acids used in the lower school, from ages 11 to 14, are very dilute indeed and even at GCSE level or equivalent, they're not much more concentrated.

The trickiest accident I encountered was something which should have been pretty innocuous. Using a Bunsen burner to heat a liquid in a glass beaker. I cannot even remember what liquid exactly.

Occasionally the Bunsen burners would get blocked, as the adorable children would drop splints down the barrel deliberately, or accidentally get wax or other particles into the barrel. The Science technicians would try to keep them as clean as possible, but it wasn't always realistic to do that every week. Nonetheless, a quick blow through of air into the barrel or into the air-hole would usually dislodge anything stuck in there. Then a few taps on the safety mat and the Bunsen would be as clean as a toot. Almost. The German chemist Robert Bunsen in 1855 at the University of Heidelberg, didn't envisage I imagine, that his simple design would still be in use in the 2020s. The best designs are always the simplest.

There is some evidence that Bunsen by the way, adapted his design from a similar design by the British scientist Michael Faraday some years earlier.

For some reason, on this particular afternoon Year 10 pupil Lacey, decided to get a closer look at what might possibly be blocking the air-hole or even the barrel of her Bunsen.

I didn't see the incident, but she somehow managed to get one of her false eyelashes trapped in the metal air-hole ring of the Bunsen and then started yelping for help as it was pulling on her eyelid. One might usually expect the false eyelash to pull off her eyelid, but in this case it didn't!

Maybe she had used superglue and I wouldn't be at all surprised.

On one noteworthy occasion, in a different school, a Year 9 girl came into school after a particularly hot and sunny June weekend, sporting a seriously scorched countenance. So painful and severe she had been taken to hospital for a check-up on the Sunday morning and to get something to palliate her sore skin. She told me on Monday morning, that she had used olive oil on her face, arms and neck and then sat out in the direct sunlight in her back garden.

"It was **virgin** olive oil" she insisted as I screwed up my face in a grimace and covered my eyes, genuinely shocked at how she had harmed her face. I've been burned by the sun often enough to know how painful it can be!

'I love the sun but it don't love me.' Is that a song title?

We obviously hadn't taught her about the EM spectrum at that point!

Most schools will allow face make-up for girls in Year 10 and above and no doubt boys as well now.

I cannot understand why a minority of girls and probably increasing numbers of boys, have to paint up their eyes, eyelashes and especially eyebrows to such an extent. It makes them look like clowns quite honestly. There is something called the 'scouse brow', of which I take personal offense, having been born in Liverpool! A very thick brow is exaggerated by dark pencil. Most often totally out of proportion to the size of the girl's face! Making the young lady look like a cross between Groucho Marx and a Welsh terrier. Add to that, matching false eyelashes a camel in a sandstorm would appreciate!

I have often bitten the inside of my cheek in an effort not to laugh. It does nothing for the average teenage girl. Nor for the not so average. Quite the opposite. I realise that teens must experiment, but seriously, can't someone have a quiet word?

Surely it would be possible to have a simple make-up class in Year 10.

Just one hour on how......well…. less is more!

Evils

I always got butterflies at the start of a new academic year. What sort of classes would I get? How would they behave? Would I be able to motivate all of them sufficiently? What would they think of me if I hadn't taught them before?

A mixture of curiosity and apprehension and hope!

I would be with these classes for 10 months.

I took over the teaching of a Year 11 class, 11R2, mixed ability, which had previously been taught as 10R2 by Mr. Robinson. He had retired at the end of the previous summer term and as far as I could see from their marks in Year 10, he had handed over a good and solid position, in preparation for GCSE's the following summer.

Laurel was a pupil I had taught way back in Year 7 and not since as far as I could remember, so at least three years previously. Which is a lifetime at that age!

Moving from an 11-year-old to a 15-year-old, going on 16.

In my first lesson with 11R2, I thought I detected a degree of animosity radiating from the newly presented Laurel of Year 11.

Halfway through the first lesson I knew that something was wrong. She was giving me evils!

'Evils' was a term for a hostile facial expression directed at another person with attending glare.

As in "Can you tell her Sir, she's been giving me 'evils' all lesson"

or "I'm just telling you Sir, he's been giving me 'evils' at break and I'm not havin it"

Laurel, who had been a reasonable but lazy student as an 11-year-old, was definitely giving me evils. It didn't help that she was at the back of the classroom and glaring at me in an antagonistic fashion every time she lifted her head from her exercise book.

Had I said something to upset her? Was she hoping for a different teacher in Year 11?

I really couldn't work it out. At the end of the lesson, I asked her to wait behind briefly with a friend of hers so I could quickly try and find out what had happened.

She was clearly brooding about something, and I only had a couple of minutes to try and find out what, before the next class were due. They were already lining up in the corridor

"Laurel, nice to see you again. Didn't I teach you in Year 7?"

Nothing.

"Er well, have I upset you in some way? You don't seem comfortable. Is something bothering you?"

"You gave me detention in Year 7 for not doing my homework! She blurted out angrily training a chipped fingernail at me. "And you rang home!"

She then turned smartly and stomped out of my classroom pulling her friend with her. Who also gave me a glower for good luck.

"That was three years ago Laurel!" I shouted after her, but she was long gone.

Maybe closer to four years, I whispered to myself.

She'd been harbouring resentment for that long?

Over that? I couldn't quite believe it!

Blindingly Obvious

H aving worked in upward of a hundred secondary schools and a few primary schools over the years, it is extraordinary how many manufacturers have not managed to find childproof window blinds! Children are often clumsy and especially teenagers going through the 'growth spurt.' Maybe adding a millimetre to each limb every week! It is sometimes difficult for them to judge distance.

Put that together with their general lack of interest in anyone else's property apart from their own. It adds up to window blinds not fit for purpose. Mangled cords, snapped cords, gaping tears in the blinds, blinds that won't raise, blinds that won't descend and generally dysfunctional window coverings. Window blinds are important in a classroom for showing video clips, or the visual effects of light experiments in science labs. Sometimes just blocking out the bright sunshine, yes, we do get it more often than we think in the UK, even on cold days, so that people can actually see images on the interactive whiteboards at the front of the classroom. Just simply so the sun isn't in the eyes of pupils, or the temperature of the room doesn't go too high.

I was in such a classroom today, the window blinds almost unrecognisable, hanging in tatters and shreds over the windows. It was a gloomy overcast day this time, with too little light in the room and it was a little bit depressing. However, try as I might, I couldn't lift the blinds in order to allow some more natural lighting into the classroom.

I've seen, I would imagine, almost every possible design of window blind. Venetian type blinds. Vertical strip blinds and plain roller blinds. All sorts of colours, materials and all sorts of designs and yet I've not seen any that work in a secondary school environment. In other words are durable enough to withstand the use in a classroom!

Teenagers are often a bit rough and as I said before quite clumsy unintentionally.

Sometimes even intentionally.

There must be a huge market out there for someone to design a durable hard working and simple window blind system for schools to use. Most schools have spent vast sums of money buying in big-ticket costly smartboards for each classroom. They are fantastically innovative if used properly, but then why not have functioning window blinds, which allow pupils to SEE the boards clearly and easily.

Why hasn't it been done? It's a mystery, there must be a lot of money to be made. It cannot be beyond the wit of design and engineer specialists to come up with product that works and will survive heavy usage in the typical school classroom. Any takers?

On the subject of school facilities, I have only once caused an entire school to be evacuated. Once was enough. Forgetting to keep the room well ventilated, in other words, every single window open, as well as the door. I learned my lesson the hard way.

15 sets of pupil pairs, burning anything on a Bunsen burner is going to cause smoke and sure, the smoke alarm did go off, setting off the fire alarm and about 1200 students had to march out of the various school buildings to the playground and sports field and line up to be registered again. Luckily the fire brigade was warned not to arrive and it went down as a successful annual fire drill, which schools are legally obliged to complete. I was not popular with the rest of the staff that day, but strangely popular with the students.

Toothurty and In the Pink

There has been a large increase in students from Eastern Europe and other parts of the world in the last few years and this can create additional problems for teaching students. The EAL capacity of some schools has had to increase significantly. (English as an additional language). On the plus side, many of the adults from the same families are more than happy to be used as Learning Support Assistants (LSA's), in schools, to assist with the new intakes. Many are very well qualified and some perhaps overqualified, but happy for such an opening for a short time at least.

In general, and regardless of whether a class is taught in rows facing the teacher or in table groups, there comes a time when a teacher must have all students facing the front and looking at the whiteboard or equivalent. I nearly came unstuck by doing what I thought was the right thing in a class of Year 10 students.

Katya was a girl from Romania who had arrived in Year 8 and had picked up her English language skills very quickly indeed, so much so, that now in Year 10 she had a boyfriend, Eddie, who was quite a bit older at 20.

I recognised him as an ex-pupil. She lived with her grandmother, not far from school, as her parents were still working in Romania. When her grandmother came to parents evening, the conversation had to proceed via Katya herself, as her gran was not at all fluent in English and we wondered just how much of the conversation was being translated accurately to and from her gran by her 15 year old granddaughter!

A comment such as

'Katya needs to improve her punctuality to school and must improve the standard of her homework being submitted', could well have been translated by Katya as:

"Katya is an excellent student, and her homework assignments are truly remarkable". For all we knew!

One of the Romanian parents I knew, Nadia, was well qualified and had not one but two degrees. I asked the Headteacher if she could be taken on as a part time role at least.

After all the DBS checking was completed, Nadia was taken on as an LSA and she proved remarkably useful, not only in helping pupils, but in liaising with parents who had sometimes very poor English.

Katya came into my lesson one day clearly wearing an almost fluorescent pink bra under her white school blouse. She was quite well developed for her age and the very noticeable pink bra was causing a ripple of attention and distraction amongst the Year 10 boys.

Apart from being not school uniform, it was ridiculously visible.

This was the last lesson of the day and after school I saw Nadia, the LSA, in the corridor and asked her if, to avoid embarrassment, she could ring Katya's gran and explain, woman to woman, in her own language, why the luminous pink bra was inappropriate.

Nadia did this within half an hour and reported back to me that the matter had been dealt with and that gran was very receptive and extremely pleased that the school had telephoned to consult with her.

One of the advantages for teachers of mobile phones is that parents or carers are much easier to contact now by mobile phone or email direct to their phone.

The next day Katya presented without the said undergarment glowing through her school blouse and we heard no more about it.

However, about a month later I had a terrible toothache which turned into a root canal treatment at a later date. The only appointment I could get was at 2.30pm. Yes, really. Well, someone must have that time slot! Toothurty. Which would mean missing the last lesson. The Deputy Principal, Mrs Samuels gave me permission to miss the last lesson and I said I would be back at school for an after-school meeting. Off I went to the dentist which was only a 15-minute walk away and I got some relief for my throbbing toothache.

As luck would have it, I ended up walking back to the school at the end of the school day, as students were pouring out of the gates and going in different directions to their homes. Very close to the school I was accosted by Katya's boyfriend who as I explained was considerably older than her and in front of all the other students he shouted at me,

"Oi!, what you doing looking at my girlfriends bra?"

Obviously out of context it didn't sound good and pupils passing were smiling and smirking. There was little I could say without making the matter worse. Especially as the boyfriend looked pretty spaced out on something. I suppose I could have asked him an obvious question,

"What is a 20-year-old doing going out with a 15 year old girl?"

Nevertheless I didn't want to have a slanging match in the street, so I just turned on my heels, said nothing and smartly walked back into school for my meeting.

So, my attempt at getting communication, woman to woman, between our Romanian LSA and the Romanian grandmother, had clearly blown up in my face.

'One can't do right for doing wrong', as I often heard, growing up in Yorkshire.

At least my actual face was less inflamed by my tooth abscess as now it had been drained.

Having a root canal procedure really does indicate why dentists are called dental surgeons. It is extremely fine detailed surgery to clean and fill root canals!

An interesting development linked to the advance of academies and academy chains is that many are offering a private healthcare, (light version) for their teaching and non-teaching staff. As most teachers are at work by that time, it means they may not have to indulge in the morning 8am scramble of sitting on the phone for an hour, trying to get a GP appointment. A humiliating ceremony which has persisted for over two decades under Labour, LibDem and Conservative governments and is an extraordinary way of treating customers who are paying taxes for the service!

50% Well Done

S chool sports day is often a mixed blessing. It's good that for one time during the school year the PE department are in charge and all things sport wise are celebrated. Sports days are usually held in the last week of the summer term or possibly the penultimate week. July in England and Wales. Scottish youngsters are already on the beaches by then! To get an entire school out onto the sports field is a logistical nightmare for a primary school and for a secondary school it is a titanic task.

1000 to 1500 students in one place, sometimes more, plus teaching and non-teaching staff. Like the Titanic it can metaphorically descend rapidly.

There is, of course, the great British weather. Weather forecasts for two or three days ahead are getting increasingly reliable now in 2023, however a sports day has to be planned probably months in advance. A day blocked out of the academic calendar. Usually an ice cream van booked or burger van or both. Well, it IS only one day per year! So, if the day has been booked so far in advance, the weather really has to be fair. If it's raining anything other than a very light rain, then it can't happen. Cannot take place indoors. Game over. Some years ago we only had to worry about rain, but nowadays it can even be too hot or too sunny.

One occasion, in a large city secondary school, we had a sports day which turned out to be the hottest day of the year. This was back in the 1990s when weather forecasts were not quite as reliable! All students were advised to bring a hat and sunscreen, plentiful drinking water would be provided. On tap.

Sports day is also the one day in the year when teachers spend the whole day with their own form groups and other pastoral staff. Most of the rest of the year, teachers work closely in subject departments or faculties. It's interesting to see students intermingling in their year groups and form-groups for a few hours solid.

There was a clear timetable for the day and it was due to run from 9:00 AM to 3:00 PM so it was a full and detailed schedule of track and field. Azure skies promised an exceptional day.

For the first hour it's a bit of a novelty for the students, so they're pretty well occupied and focused on the events, as they sit around the track watching races and other events in the centre of the running track. For the other five hours the teachers and other staff have to be alert and very much on their toes to keep the students focused as they can get increasingly restless. Its vital that there is a good sound system set up so that ALL students and staff can hear what is going on and keep up interest in the events. A good MC is also needed on the microphone. Sadly, all too often the sound system is not fit for purpose and students lose interest swiftly, as they gradually miss track of what's going on. Excuse the pun. The previous year the sound system was very temperamental and kept cutting out and then back on for no discernible reason.

The MC that year was a drama teacher, Mr Cardwell, who was doing well pumping up the children and creating a bit of, well, drama, when the microphone cut out for the umpteenth time. His normal phlegmatic manner was getting profoundly tested.

The Headteacher, Mrs Walker, on one of her visits to the sports field, cupped her hands and shouted in his direction.

"Mr Cardwell, project your voice!"

A gauntlet unintentionally laid down for any honourable drama teacher!

Mr Cardwell, who obviously thought the microphone was in its off mode, could be clearly heard saying.

"Come over here and I will stick this microphone up your arse Mrs Walker"

Cue, a strange silence descending on the field of play for a few moments.

Another year, the headteacher had decided the sports day would finish with a different fun event, as selected students would try to soak teachers in temporary 'stocks' that the woodwork department had crafted. Students would buy a raffle ticket for 50p which went to charity and then students whose names were selected from a hat, would be allowed to soak a large sponge in buckets of cold water and aim them at a teacher 'in the stocks'. What could possibly go wrong? Well, nothing as it turned out because the event didn't occur.

There were whispers going around the previous day that certain of the more spiteful students were going to try and secrete stones and rocks in the sponges! Whether this was true or not the headteacher decided to abandon the event in the face of staff discontent and possibly serious injuries.

Despite telling my own form group, 8F, to bring a hat and sunscreen to the event, I stupidly didn't take my own advice. I rushed out of the house in the morning to get to school, convinced I had left a wide brimmed hat and sunscreen in the boot of my car. I hadn't.

As the day wore on and all the teachers and support staff were effectively standing in the same direction, around the marked out grassy track, there was little to no shade from the sun. The following day I was sporting a very sunburnt half of my face on the right-hand side, but the left side was my typically pallid anaemic looking colour! Almost as if someone had drawn a pencil down my forehead, along my nose and down my chin. I looked pretty ridiculous and it would take a few days to settle. Novice mistake. Never underestimate the strength of the giant hydrogen bomb in the sky!

I've never fully fathomed the news stories and comments about schools not having competitive sports days. I've worked in 8 large secondary schools full time and many more schools on supply since and I have never, ever come across a secondary school that didn't have an extremely competitive sports day and sports fixtures programmed across the whole year. The only exception being during Covid19 pandemic.

Whiteboard Communication and Other Rants

As a supply teacher since I retired and working through various agencies and in dozens and dozens of secondary schools, it has shocked me how poorly supply teachers are sustained and supported to deliver lessons in schools. It is a great mystery to me. Schools are paying upwards of £200 a day for a supply teacher, each and every day, if you include the teacher supply agency fee. Even more in London.

Conversing with other supply teachers as we bump into each other in different schools at lunchtime and so on, my experience is very typical from what I'm told.

It seems that all the Outstanding, Grade 1 Ofsted schools have one thing in common, they give supply teachers the tools to deliver in the classroom at the chalk face. OK, chalk has long gone, but the classroom is where the teaching and learning takes place!

An appropriately prepared supply teacher would have been given on arrival, a laptop with the means to access student information such as the critical SEND (Special Educational Needs) information. Hard copy lesson plans, or access to electronic lesson plans. Student thumbnail photos, so the supply teacher can identify QUICKLY the students in each class. It's necessary to move fast and identify any possible disruptive students and sit on them metaphorically. All the rest of the information in outstanding schools is given usually in a properly prepared booklet, Safeguarding Lead teachers with photos, a clear and simple Sanctions and Rewards policy.

Yes, and Rewards! A Fire Drill plan and map of the school are given in almost all schools. A map, why? There are literally hundreds of students who are happy, quickly and succinctly to give you directions when they see your ID lanyard.

Many schools are paying considerable sums of money from the annual school budget for supply teachers, yet they often set up a supply teacher to fail. Over and over again.

Very few schools expect the supply teacher to use the Rewards ladder. This is critical or else the supply teacher is always seen in a very negative light and only ever using a sanctions system. Most schools will have a published Sanctions and Rewards system.

"Oh, you'll need the Sanctions ladder as you will probably need it" I'm told on arrival, with good intentions no doubt.

Yes, maybe. However, if schools assume supply teachers will have difficulties in a classroom, then difficulties will happen, as that attitude filters through to the students' mindsets.

Most issues are caused by teachers not being able to identify any challenging students. (No photos!). The students know this and will play up.

An out-of-date seating plan and very often no seating plan at all. If I had a pound for every time a class told me this:

"Yeah, that seating plan is out of date Sir".

"Miss/Sir changed it a couple of weeks ago".

The sound of a rug being pulled out from under me is thunderous. Every time.

I have a choice, either to enforce the seating plan I've been given, (if any) and end up with serious confrontation with some individual students, thus wasting learning time or accepting where the students have chosen to sit and proceeding with the lesson.

The chances are very high that the seating plan IS out of date.

Whenever I have handed in some feedback at the end of the day for each class, I am usually met with astonishment that I used the Rewards system, assuming I could find it. Yet, most excellent students just want to learn and make progress. Why can't supply teachers be allowed to recognise that formally?

Now onto whiteboards! Most classrooms will have an electronic whiteboard which often a supply teacher cannot use because they haven't been given a laptop or access. Plus, a 'dumb' whiteboard for writing on with whiteboard marker pens.

Very many of these 'dumb' whiteboards are covered in ink from previously wiped-out lessons, so as to make them almost unreadable. We are in the business of communication! Even the most literate of students will struggle to read from these murky, blotchy, mottled, greyed-out indistinct whiteboards! They are rarely properly white! Some students are below their expected reading ages in the first place. So why make it harder for them to follow the lesson?

The teachers are frequently too busy to really give the whiteboards a good clean at least once a week, so why not assign a cleaner to properly clean these boards weekly, to prevent build-up of ink. The floors are clean daily, the desks are cleaned daily. The bins are emptied daily. The toilets are cleaned daily. Why not give some TLC to the neglected whiteboard? Communication is key.

A trick I found when Head of Science, was to put a very fine layer of WD40 on the 'dumb' whiteboards, AFTER they have been cleaned. It stops the ink sinking into the board. Does anyone know why it is called WD40? It was the 40th attempt by the inventor in San Diego California to get the formula just right to make a product for water displacement, hence WD. Useless but interesting bit of trivia.

Finally, schools should be expecting feedback from supply teachers, positive and negative, and then ensuring that gets fed into the school systems, so students know it is worth their while engaging and doing the right thing even when their lesson is being covered.

Turning A Corner

It was in one of the training schools during my teacher training course, that I realised why the Germans are far better at long term planning in industry than other countries. Although the recent reliance on Russian gas pipelines might indicate they are losing their skills of foresight.

The school was in the midlands and in fact was the largest employer in that market town. A large German yoghurt manufacturer decided to build a brand-new factory just outside the town to meet growing demand in the UK market. They had worked out pretty easily that they could get enough milk from within about a 50-mile radius of their new plant. From North Wales, Cheshire and Staffordshire. Plenty of dairy farms and good quality milk.

They then turned their attention to their future workforce and wrote to the school asking if they could have a meeting with the Head of Science and Head of Biology. The company were interested in how the students at the school were being taught microbiology in the lower and upper school.

Its lucky they didn't look inside the Head of Biology's coffee cup!

They weren't looking for graduates necessarily for the future, obviously they would recruit direct from Universities. They were thinking however, of future skilled technicians, who would have a basic understanding of food hygiene and microbes. That really is forward planning.

Which reminds me, I often did an experiment on aseptic technique at GCSE.

Students using a metal loop sterilised in the ubiquitous Bunsen flame and then doing a sweep of a surface and transferring any invisible microbes that were present, onto the surface of sterilised agar jelly in a petri dish.

Every time I did this procedure I asked for volunteers to do a quick sweep of a toilet seat nearby. We left the petri dishes alone for a few days and then examined the dishes. Without exception, the dirtiest parts of the classroom were the door handles and window handles, the cleanest area was ALWAYS the toilet seat! Not surprising really as it was disinfected every day! This linked up nicely with the accepted theory that the original SARS virus in February 2003 was transmitted within a conference hotel in Hong Kong by people touching contaminated elevator buttons. The 2003 outbreak, which thankfully did not turn into a Pandemic was the warning siren which most governments failed to heed.

I was always a bit anxious that in the Biology GCSE class we might accidentally release a germ as yet unknown to humankind.

This was years before Covid19, so don't blame me.

Mrs Delaney and Josh

C heryl Delaney came into the staffroom eating a piece of toast and spraying crumbs in front of her. It was 7.55am and as Head of Year she already had taken a call patched through to the staffroom from the Heads PA, from the store manager of a large ASDA store around the corner from the school.

The store manager was not happy that one of our pupils had already been caught shoplifting clothes from the store at just before 7.30am and another pupil had 'fessed up' as they say, to identify the lad as a Year 9 boy.

"I haven't even finished my breakfast and they're on my case" she despaired.

This is before a full day of teaching and probably an after-school meeting.

It wouldn't take too long to identify the pupil, as children are remarkably loquacious most of the time.

By lunchtime she had narrowed it down to Josh Lindon, a small but loud and problematic boy. She tackled him with the Deputy Head at the start of lunchtime and he denied all knowledge of the incident, let alone tell her where the stolen clothes had been hidden, probably in a nearby hedge to be collected after school.

Exasperated she decided to call his bluff and she and the deputy head Mr Carmichael frogmarched Josh out of the school around the corner, across the traffic lights, at which point Mrs Delaney was seriously wondering if she had got the wrong pupil.

"The store manager says you're caught on CCTV Josh, so I don't know why you're making us go through all this nonsense" she proclaimed.

"It will either be you on the camera or not, if it's not, I'll apologise, but you and I both know it was you." She was having doubts.

Josh kept a tempo with the two teachers on either side of him, with an air of determined grievance. A young person insulted and wrongfully accused. His chin was jutted out in resolve and martyrdom.

As they got nearer to the superstore's automatic entrance, now only a few metres away, the two teachers looked down to find Josh literally walking backwards as they were still walking forwards.

"Okay oh my days", he grumbled, "it was me, Terry made me do, he told me we could sell them on, next Saturday at market".

Mrs Delaney and Mr Carmichael stopped walking, one looking up at the sky in real weariness, the other shaking her head looking at Josh's unembarrassed countenance. They turned around and took him back to school.

"Why make us walk all the way over here Josh?" said Mrs Delaney with frustration.

The offending items were recovered, and Josh took his punishment like the little boy he was and sobbed manfully as his Mum came to pick him up from school for his two day exclusion. Mrs Delaney missed lunch as well as breakfast. She was carrying a few extra pounds anyway, so she named it "the tea-leaf diet."

It is amazing how a few children can brazenly tell cold lies whilst keeping perfect eye contact. A fact I've never really comprehended.

Primary Return

After retirement, I worked for various agencies on a daily basis. Usually secondary, as I was obviously trained as a secondary school teacher.

I think the PGCE course was titled Broad Balanced Science. Basically, a way of getting Physics graduates to teach Bio and Chemistry and Biology graduates to teach the other two etc. In any case I refused all offers to do a day in a primary school until one day I got a desperate call from an agency at 7.15 am.

"Mark can you PLEASE, I am begging you, do a day in St Peters Primary. They are desperate and I've used all my primary supply staff. The school just rang in 5 minutes ago. They're really desperate. Its Year 2. All the work will be set".

Setting aside the notion that I was the desperate choice, I agreed, provided they paid me a bit extra for the petrol.

"Oh, thank you so much Mark. They'll be relieved. I owe you one, I'll text the details now to you."

So how bad could it be? A day of supply with 6-year-olds. Might be a pleasant change!

I showered, had breakfast standing up and 5 minutes later was in my car. Satnav set to the texted postcode. Yes of course I brushed my teeth! Or toothypegs as I was beginning to think of them. Got to get into the mindset of a six year old…..

I arrived and showed my DBS Certificate and photo ID as is quite rightly standard procedure and was taken to the classroom with more exclamations of gratitude that I had been able to cover the day. Two teachers off sick and another teacher's wife had gone into labour in the wee hours. (Why do we call it the wee hours?) Three teaching staff off school, that's a lot for a Primary.

My first surprise was that I wasn't covering Year 2 but Year 1.

5-year-olds rather than 6-year-olds. Oh well. I had my suspicions that the agency had tricked me, knowing Year 1 would be pushing it, to sell to me at 07.15 am. Maybe it was a genuine mistake.

Pleasingly there was an LSA, (Learning Support Assistant) present in the classroom setting up resources for the day. Some schools use the term TA or teaching assistant. In essence, the same role. Avril, a middle-aged lady with a posh Geordie accent was welcoming and reassuring.

"Oh, they'll be fine pet, its Friday, they'll be a bit hyper for the weekend but cracking just the same" Well, being so far south has smoothed her accent I thought.

"How long you been down here Avril?"

"Nigh on 30 year now pet."

"Same, I'm from Leeds." I declared.

"Wow you don't sound like a yorkie."

Chit-chat over as the parents and youngsters were rearing into vision outside the classroom windows.

The order of the day was as follows.

Literacy 1 hour
Numeracy 1 hour
Break or playtime outside.
Science (yea, my subject) 1 hour
Lunchtime
Afternoon. Reading a reading book. Aloud by me.
Drawing
I must have missed something out, probably PE.

Besides, the day was going fine and the LSA was brilliant helping me and pointing out issues that I would be unaware of, e.g., Mikey always tries to wind up Alison in numeracy. Which pupils should be sitting at each table and so on. Invaluable knowledge to a teacher and even more so to a supply teacher who doesn't know the pupils by name or disposition.

So far so good. I got through to lunchtime. We got there.

Avril reminded me to leave 10 full minutes to get them packed away and to put on their outdoor coats. She was utterly spot on. It took 10 full minutes and a bit more.

Sadly, Avril Lee only worked part time. Mornings only, which took me a bit by surprise.

At lunchtime I ate my second cereal bar of the day and got a cup of tea from the miniature staffroom.

Afternoon session and no LSA. I had forlornly expected another LSA to turn up for the afternoon session. However, I was honestly expecting I might be on my own.

I presumed well. With 30 wriggling 5-year-olds increasingly excited about the upcoming weekend.

So, we started off reading aloud a story. I asked them to recap it for me, up to the point they got to the previous day. A good bit of recall literacy, comprehension and listening skills. It also gave me an impression of what the story was about. A crafty frog apparently.

Then things started to go wrong. After what seemed like 30 minutes, it may have been less, the children started to get restless. So, onto drawing. A nice easy end to the week. Hopefully.

I had forgotten how needy 5-year-olds are, despite having three children myself. I was shocked by how many needed to show me and get approval from me, at regular intervals of 5 minutes. I decided to sit down at the teachers' desk and look at one boys drawing.

As if by magic, as I was looking down for maybe 20 seconds, a line of children lined up behind him! Half the class just left their seats and strangely, silently started to queue behind Bobby. Really rather creepy. Who knew a bunch of five-year-olds could move so quietly yet quickly? They all wanted my critique of their, maybe at most, 15 minutes artwork.

Rather overwhelmed, but a bit fatigued by now and a little irritated. I managed to keep my voice light and fluffy and asked all the children in the queue to hold up their drawings for me. They did so and I pronounced them all superb. They were happy with that, and all raced back to their table groups to continue. Phew. Mini crisis averted.

Come back Avril! I thought I'd broken the back of the afternoon, when disaster! Rosie came up to me sobbing and crying. Her little shoulders jumping up and down with each sob. I was devastated. What could have happened?

I envisaged social services having to be called. Me writing incident reports until well into the night. I just could not imagine what had upset her so very much. The rest of the class carried on regardless, quite happily drawing. That should have been a clue.

I eventually got Rosie to stop sobbing long enough to speak to me.

She held up her drawing for me to inspect. I looked.

It was an animal, possibly. They were all supposed to be drawing animals. I said, "But why are you crying Rosie? This is lovely". Whatever it was.

In-between now less frequent sobs she explained.

"Joseph said my horse looked like a pig". Oh, I see. I pretended to assess the rogue drawing more closely. "Nope, Rosie that is most definitely a beautiful horse. Well done!"

She stopped sobbing instantly. Instantly! She returned skipping back to her table. A vision of happiness and content as if a new artist just accepted at the Royal Academy.

The rest of the session proceeded calmly. Joseph giving me side-glances of a slight smirk and yet approval.

Then it was home time. I'd forgotten Mrs Lee's 10-minute instruction. We packed away in a hurry. I could see parents beginning to arrive for collection. Luckily an LSA from another class came in.

"Have you checked your collection folder?" I feigned cluelessness. She took a folder from the desk and gave it to me. Next to each child's name was a parent or other responsible adult who was permitted to collect them from school. So going home time was not just a flash of flinging open the door and saying, have a nice weekend. They were counted in and each one had to be counted out.

I have to say I slept very soundly that night. Utterly and completely exhausted.

I think I prefer a boisterous group of Year 11 students.

About the Author

Mark MacDonald has been a Secondary School Science teacher in England U.K. for 33 years. He has been Head of Year, Head of Science, Assistant Headteacher as well as a School Governor in three different schools.

Before teaching he worked for Adults with Learning Difficulties for 3 years for a local authority in Wales and a charity in France.

He has three adult daughters. He has travelled quite widely with his family around Europe, the USA and South America as well as India, Hong Kong, Mauritius, the Caribbean and Australia. His favourite country is probably Australia with Peru and India close seconds.